Chertsey and its neighbourhood.

S C. Hall

Chertsey and its neighbourhood.
Hall, S C.
British Library, Historical Print Editions
British Library
1853
iv. 64 p. ; 8º.

CHERTSEY

AND ITS NEIGHBOURHOOD.

By MRS. S. C. HALL.

— K

PRINTED AND SOLD FOR THE BENEFIT OF THE INFANT SCHOOL
AT ADDLESTONE.

1853.

LONDON:
BRADBURY AND EVANS, PRINTERS, WHITEFRIARS.

LIST OF ILLUSTRATIONS.

CHERTSEY AND ITS NEIGHBOURHOOD.

"Come now toward Chertsey."—*Richard the Third.*

ONE of the most pleasurable sensations of life arises from the consciousness of an increasing attachment, not only to the land we live in, but to our own immediate neighbourhood. We confess to the possession of a large organ of inhabitiveness; and can sympathise with the cat, the beaver,—even with the crow, who prefers repairing his old ricketty nest to building a new one. 'Exile!' has ever seemed to us the most fearful of all punishments; and the power to augment the enjoyments and endear the associations of 'home,' one of earth's greatest blessings; but when that 'home' is placed in a locality, where time and its memories sanctify the beauties of nature, and every walk or drive is suggestive of something which recals either history or legend, the interest increases daily, until we seem to claim actual acquaintance with those whom we can summon from amid the shadows of the past. So much has been done, so many scenes have been enacted, such numberless great men have lived and died within this small but mighty England, that every rood of ground, so to say, has its story; and it needs but small imagination to derive profitable instruction from highways and byways in any shire of our island.

The county of Surrey, so closely connected with London, is rich to overflowing in all sorts of memories, both of persons and events; and the little quaint and quiet town of Chertsey with its 'grants,' and 'fairs,' and 'markets,'—which to judge by its usual state of sleepy tranquillity seem to be rather fanciful than real—that very discreet little town could tell of the gorgeous and gloomy past, as much as, or perhaps more than, many of its ancient neighbours within a day's drive of the Metropolis. Had the old Abbey stones (out of which, according to tradition, the walls of sundry of its now meek-looking houses were raised)—had they but tongues, how they could discourse of gone-by years—when a visit to Chertsey was an undertaking; although now, the distance between the city and the town is just an hour.

We hear as we enter our house (in Addlestone, one of its tributary villages) the curfew-bell, tolling as in 'the good old times,' when people dared not 'show' in the street after its last peal had sounded. The curfew has endured in spite of all 'reforms'—at once a relic and a reminder of ancient days, when it rung, as it does now, from Michaelmas to Lady-day, at eight of the evening. The worthy sexton of Chertsey first 'rings up,' that is to say, raises the bell; he then rings for a few minutes, and stops a little while; after which he tolls the number of the day of the month; on the first day of the month, he strikes the bell once, and on the last day thirty or thirty-one times.*

* The generally received opinion that the ringing of the curfew-bell and the consequent compulsory extinguishing of fire and candle, was imposed on the English by William the Conqueror as a badge of servitude, is open to considerable doubt, inasmuch as a similar law existed in other parts of Europe as a necessary safeguard at a period when houses were constructed of wood, and huddled together in walled towns. It is even stated that Alfred the Great, one of our most popular sovereigns, introduced the usage. That it was neither so odious nor unpopular as the Poet Thomson vividly describes it to have been, (and from whose lines probably most persons form their idea,) is apparent from the fact of private individuals in the middle ages frequently leaving sums of money toward defraying the expenses of ringing it, and keeping it in repair. In flat, marshy, and dangerous places it was an useful guide by night to the traveller. The curfew or *couvre-feu* itself was a metal instrument so contrived that it covered in and extinguished the whole of the wood fire on the hearth when it was raked to the back of the chimney. They are among the rarest of our domestic antiquities, being of that class which when out of fashion is soonest consigned to the melting-pot. Horace Walpole had one at Strawberry Hill; another is engraved in Hone's 'Every-day-book;' and a third in the Journal of the British Archæological Association.

Chertsey is described in county histories as a 'neat market-town on the north side of Surrey, twenty miles from London;' it is singularly 'neat' and clean and quiet; nothing within our memory has occurred to disturb its tranquillity. The name was written occasionally in old chronicles, *Cirolesege*, *Certessege*, or *Ceroti Insula*. Its situation may be said to be insular; the Thames and Abbey river being on one side, and on the other a small stream, now known as the Bourne, which comes in a leisurely dreamy way from Virginia Water on its passage to the Thames.

Chertsey has also a branch railroad—our especial own—from Weybridge, with a station at the ambitious village of Addlestone.* The railroad partakes of the nature of the neighbourhood; not being by any means busy or boisterous, and having in an out-of-the-way corner of the pretty quiet town, a little low-shed terminus which seems as if it had no business there, and inclines to apologise for its intrusion; yet this absence of puff and noise on the part of the railroad, this intense quiet, is in admirable keeping with the present character of the peaceful locality: the town lies low, the Thames, bright and full-bosomed as it flows, is enriched on either side by the greenest and most verdant meadows. In the season you are certain to see many contemplative brothers of the angle engaged at their 'idle industry,' either along the banks or in unpicturesque boats—boats which sleep lazily among rushes, until the first of June calls them from their rest. But to write more seriously, nowhere, within twenty miles of London (except in the immediate neighbourhood of Richmond) does the bland and beautiful Thames appear more queenly, or sweep with greater grace through its fertile dominions, than it does at Chertsey. It is, indeed, delightful to stand on the bridge in the glowing sunset of a summer evening, and, turning from the refreshing green of the Shepperton Range, look into the deep clear blue of the flowing river, while the murmurs of the waters rushing through Laleham Lock give a sort of Spirit-music to the scene. On the right, as you leave

* There are few villages in England more healthily circumstanced than Addlestone; on an elevated flat, upon a fine gravel soil, neither damps nor exhalations are ever seen there. Free currents of pure air are seldom interrupted by trees. The views, although there are none from the immediate village, are of singular beauty and extent in the neighbourhood. The village is scattered; there are about two hundred houses, yet no ten of them are together.

Chertsey, the river bends gracefully towards the double bridge of Walton; and to the left, it undulates smoothly along, having passed Runnymead and Staines, while the almost conical hill of St. Anne's attracts attention by its abrupt form when viewed from the vale of the Thames.

Nor must we forget that, about a mile on the Walton side, from our favourite bridge (Old Camden tells us so), are the 'Cowey Stakes,' marking the spot where Cæsar crossed the Thames.

Were the peasantry of Surrey and Middlesex as imaginative as their Irish brethren of Killarney, what legends would have grown out of this tradition; how often would the 'noblest Roman of them all' have been seen by the pale moonlight leading his steed over the waters of the rapid river—how many would have borne testimony to the fact that Cassivelaunus himself had been heard during the stillness of some particular Midsummer night working at the rude defence which can still be traced beneath the blue waters of the Thames. What hosts of pale and ghastly spectres would have risen from those tranquil banks, and from the deepest hollows of the rushing current, and—like the Huns, who almost live on the inspired canvas of Kaulbach,—fought their last earthly battle, again, and again, in the Spirit-world, amid the stars! But ours is no region of romance; even remnants of history, which go beyond the commonest capacity, are rejected as dreams, or put aside as legends. But history has enough to tell to interest us all; and we may be satisfied with the abundant enjoyment we have in delicious rambles, through the lanes and up the hills, along the fair river's banks, and among the many traditional ruins of ancient and beautiful Surrey.

Never was desolation more complete than in the ruin of the Mitred Abbey of Chertsey; hardly one stone remains above another to tell where this stately edifice—since the far-away year 664—grew and flourished, lording it with imperial sway over, not only the surrounding villages, but extending its paternal wings into Middlesex and even as far as London.* The Abbey was of the Benedictine order, and founded almost as soon as the Saxons were converted from Paganism, by Erkenwalde, afterwards

* Stowe, in his account of the ward of Queenhithe, says, 'There is one great messuage sometime belonging to the abbots of Chertsey in Surrey; and was their home wherein they were lodged when they repayred to the Citie.'

Bishop of London; but it was finished and chiefly endowed by Frithwald, Earl of Surrey.*

The endowment prospered rarely; the establishment increased in the reputation of wealth and sanctity; that it was 'thickly populated' is certain, for when the Abbey was sacked and burnt by the Danes, in the

[illegible]

ninth century, the abbot, and ninety monks, were barbarously murdered by the invaders.

Standing upon the site of their now obliterated cloisters and towers, their aisles and dormitories, cells and confessionals, seeing nothing but the dank, damp grass, and the tracings of the fishponds—stagnant pools in our day—it is almost impossible to realise the onslaught of these wild

* Sir Edward Coke tells us, that *Saint* Erkenwalde was a younger son of Anna, king of the East Saxons, and was first Abbot of Chertsey (which he had founded) and afterwards Bishop of London.

barbarians panting for plunder, the earnest defence of men who fought (the monks of old could wield either sword or crozier) for life or death, the terrible destruction, the treasures and relics and painted glass and monuments, the plunder of the secret almerys,* the intoxicated triumph of these rude northern hordes let loose in our fair and lovely island; what scenes of savagery, where now the jackdaw builds, and the blackbird whistles, and the wild water-rat plays with her brood amongst the tangled weeds!

The fierce sea-kings being driven back to their frozen land, King Edgar, willing to serve God after the fashion of his times, refounded the Abbey of Chertsey, dedicating it to St. Peter, and vying with Pope Alexander in augmenting its privileges and its wealth.†

Some of the abbots took great interest in home improvements, planting woods, conducting streams, enlarging ponds—building, now a mill, now a dove-cot, according to the wants of the Abbey or their own fancies. Henry I. granted them permission to keep dogs, that, according to the old chronicle, they might take 'hare, fox, and cats.' King John, in the first year of his reign, gave them ample confirmation of all their privileges which, it would seem, they had somewhat abused, for we find that the sovereign seized their manors of Egham and 'Torp' (Thorpe) ‡ on account

* In the ancient Rites of Durham, frequent mention is made of the Almerys, for different purposes;—'Within the Frater House door is a strong ambrie (almery) in the stone wall, where a great mazer, called a grace-cup, did stand, which did service to the monks every day after grace was said, to drink it round the table.'

† Chertsey was one of the Mitred Abbeys, whose head was also a baron or military tenant of the crown, holding his lands by barony. It was founded in the year 666 by Frithwald, the King of Mercia's viceroy for Surrey. He endowed it largely with nine hides of land well populated; and shortly afterwards larger possessions, so that the monks increased in worldly wealth, and obtained the Pope's confirmation of their possessions. The Danes burnt their home and killed ninety of the monks; but Edward the Confessor reinstated them, and granted them Chertsey itself, Egham, Thorp, Chobham, and some adjacent villages, so that they again waxed rich; at the Conquest, William I. munificently confirmed all to them free from any tax, and gave them entire jurisdiction over their lands, indulgences which were ratified by his successors, who added many rich gifts; so that the Abbey became one of the wealthiest and most powerful in the country, remaining in quiet possession of its riches until the dissolution by Henry VIII.

‡ In the parish of Thorpe are two pieces of land called 'great and little custom pieces.' The former supplies six loads of made hay every year for the use of the queen's deer in

of a servant of the abbot's having killed 'Hugh de Torp.' Oh, rare 'old times!' The abbot was mulcted in a heavy fine. Then, while Bartholomew de Winchester was abbot, from 1272 until 1307, during the reign of our first Edward, complaints were made to Pope Gregory X. that the possessions of the Abbey were alienated to civilians and laymen, whereupon the pope issued a bull ordering such grants to be revoked.

It is worthy of note, that the Chertsey monastery sheltered, for a time, the remains of the pious but unfortunate Henry VI.—

> 'Poor key-cold figure of a Holy King,
> Pale ashes of the house of Lancaster:'

and the reader of Shakespeare will recall the scene in which Richard meets the Lady Anne on her way to Chertsey with her husband's body.

This poor king's remains had a claim to be well received by the monks of Chertsey Abbey, for he had granted to the abbot the privilege of holding a fair on St. Anne's hill, then called Mount Eldebury, on the feast of St. Anne's (the 26th of July): the fair has changed its time and quarters as well as its patron, and is held in the town on the 6th of August, and called Black Cherry Fair. Manning, in his history of Surrey, says, that the tolls of this fair were taken by the abbot, and are now taken by the owner of the site of the Abbey House; thus the memory of King Henry VI. is commemorated in the town of Chertsey to this day, by the sale of black cherries in the harvest month of August!

Centuries passed over those magnificent abbeys, whose ruins in many places add so much beauty to our fertile landscapes; they grew and grew, and added acre to acre, and stone to stone, and knowledge to knowledge; but most they cherished the knowledge which blazed like a lamp under a bushel, and kept all but themselves in darkness: they preached no freedom in Christ to the Christian world, they abolished no serfdom, they taught no liberty, they enslaved even those who in their turn enslaved

Windsor Park, to be ricked there; and Mr. Bennett, lord of the manor of Thorpe, and vicar of the parish, delivers it regularly. If the crop of the great custom piece is insufficient to supply the quantity, it is made up from the little custom piece. In return, Mr. Bennett may claim an annual buck and a fawn or two, and the right of turning out four horses in Windsor Park; the latter claim is never exercised. This information has been courteously supplied to us by the Rev. Mr. Bennett.

their 'born thralls,' and saw no evil in it. Oh, rare old times! Better is it for us that the site of Chertsey Abbey should be scarcely traceable now-a-days than that it should be as it was, with its proud pageants and pent-up learning!—Yet we have neither sympathy nor respect for that foul king, who, to serve his own carnal purposes, overthrew the very faith which had hallowed his throne. But he did not attack and storm the Abbey of Chertsey, as he did other religious houses. He came to them, this Eighth Harry, with a fair show of kindness, saying that 'to the honour of God, and for the health of his soul, he proposed and most nobly intended to refound the late Monastery, Priory, or Abbey of Bisham, in Berks, and to incorporate and establish the Abbot and Convent of Chertsey, as Abbot and Convent of Bisham, and to endow them with all the Manors late belonging to Bisham.'* How the then Abbot, John Cordrey, and his brethren, must have shivered at the conditions; how they must have grieved at quitting their cherished home, their stews and fish-ponds, their rich meadows of Thorpe, overlooked by the woods of Eldebury hill, their nursing-ground where their calves and young lambs were stowed in luxurious safety in the pleasant farm of Simple Marsh at Addlestone! †

But their star was setting, and they were forced to comply with hard conditions; here they are in one terrible sentence:—

'The Abbot and Monks of Chertsey, give, sell, grant and confirm, to the king their house and all manors belonging to them.'

The total destruction of the Abbey must have amazed the whole country; an earthquake could hardly have obliterated it more entirely. Aubrey, writing in the year 1673, says, 'of this great Abbey, scarce anything of the old building remains, except the out walls about it. Out of this ruin is built a "fair house," which is now in possession of Sir Nicholas Carew, master of the Buckhounds.' Dr. Stukeley alludes to this house, in a letter written in 1752; he speaks of the inveterate destruction,

* Bisham Abbey, on the Thames, adjacent to Great Marlow, instead of being a ruin like Chertsey, is now a fine picturesque house, of singularly venerable character: it is inhabited by one of the Members for the county.

† The farm of Simple Marsh was the endowment of the sacristan of the Abbey, and its high and healthy situation was doubtless appreciated by the monks, who must have suffered from the low and swampy situation of their Abbey.

and of 'the gardener,' carrying him through 'a court' where he saw the remains of the church of the Abbey. He says the 'east end reached up to an artificial mount along the garden wall; that mount and all the terraces of the pleasure-garden, to the back front of the house, are entirely made up of the sacred rudera or rubbish of continual devastations. Bones of abbots, monks, and great personages, who were buried in large numbers in the church and cloisters which lay on the south side of the church, were spread thick all over the garden, *so that one may pick up whole handsfull of them everywhere amongst the garden stuff.*' Brayley mentions in his pleasant History of Surrey, that this artificial mount was levelled in 1810, and its materials employed to fill up a pond. Many human skulls and bones were found intermixed with the chalk and mortar of which it had been formed. Fragments of old tiles were also frequently found, and are still sometimes turned up. No trace even of the 'Abbey house' is left; it was purchased in 1809 by a stock-broker, who in the following year sold the materials—and so ends the great monastic history of the Mitred Abbey of Chertsey. Where are now its spiritualities in Surrey?—its temporalities in Berkshire and Hampshire?—its revenues of Stanwell and rents of assize?—its spiritualities in Cardiganshire? Alas! alas! they have left no sign, except on the yellow parchment—of rare value to the antiquary.

Those who desire, like ourselves, to investigate what tradition has sanctified, will do well to turn down a lane beyond Chertsey Church,*

* Chertsey Church is of old foundation; the only external traces of antiquity are in the tower, which has remained through all changes, the upper part being repaired and heightened by bricks. Within, the chancel is old, but has been altered to adapt it to the new work with which it is conjoined. The body of the old church being greatly decayed, and of too narrow dimensions for the necessities of the parish, it was determined to rebuild it in 1806, but the expense being considerably greater than the architect's estimate, the tower and chancel were incorporated with the new work. Of the six bells contained in its tower one is said to have belonged to the Abbey; it has round its verge an inscription in early English letters, each an inch in height, as follows:—

'Ora : mente : pia. pro : nobis : Virgo : Maria.'

In a few of the windows are fragments of stained glass, but there are none of the relics of antiquity within it which gives such a charm to many of our country churches. Close to the altar-rails is a bas-relief, by Flaxman, representing the Saviour raising the daughter of Jairus. It is a group of seven small figures treated in the simple and severe style of the sculptor.

which leads directly to the Abbey bridge ; there amid tangled hedge-rows and orchards, stands the fragment of an arch, partly built up, and so to say, disfigured by brick-work, and an old wall, both evidently portions of the Abbey. In the wall are a great number of what the people call '*black stones,*' a geological formation, making them seem fused by fire. Layers of tiles were also inserted in this wall, and where the cement has dropped away they can be distinctly traced ; there is also an ivy, very aged indeed ; it is so knotted and thick that it seems to grow through the stones, the soil has so evidently encroached on the wall that it is most probably rooted at the foundation. The pleasant market-garden of Mr. Roake covers the actual ground on which the Abbey stood. The workmen frequently turn up broken tiles and human bones, and there is no doubt that by digging deeper much would be discovered that might elucidate the history of the past. At the farther end of the market-garden a vault has been discovered which is of considerable length and breadth ; but the water rises so high in it (except when a long continuance of dry weather has sealed the land springs) that it is impossible to get to the end without wading. An enormous quantity of richly-coloured and decorated encaustic tiles have been found here ; some are preserved in our local museum. But the most interesting remains in this place are the 'stews,' or fish-ponds, which run parallel to each other, like the bars of a gridiron ; these ponds do not communicate one with the other, nor has the water any outlet: a little care and attention might make them valuable for their old purposes, but they are deplorably neglected. Occasionally you see the fin of some huge fish, whose slow movement partakes of the character of the stagnant water he has inhabited for years—who can tell how many ?

'The Abbey River,' as it is still called, travels slowly along its way, fertilising the meadows and imparting life and freshness to the placid scene. The denizens of Chertsey have planted orchards, and in a few instances gardens on its banks. One, the garden of Mr. Herring, is a model of neatness, almost concealed by its roses and carefully tended shrubs. We wandered from orchard to orchard, amid the trees and over the uneven ground: all was so still and lonely, that it required the suggestions of an active imagination to believe it had ever been the scene of contention by flood and field. From the Abbey Bridge the richness of the meadow scenery is exceedingly refreshing, the grass is deep and verdant, as it cannot fail to be, lying so low, and fertilised by perpetual moisture.

During their wide-spreading magnificence, the abbots of Chertsey, erected a picturesque chapel, on the lovely hill of St. Anne: this was done somewhat about the year 1334. Orleton, Bishop of Winchester, granted an indulgence of forty days, to such persons as should repair to, and contribute to the fabric and its ornaments.

There is nowhere a more delightful road, than that which leads from the 'Golden Grove,' rendered picturesque by its old tree,* the plantations

'The Golden Grove.'

of Monksgrove on one side, and those of the once residence of Charles James Fox on the other. The road is perfectly embowered, and so close is the foliage that you have no idea of the beautiful view which awaits you, until leaving the statesman's house to the left, you pass through a sort of wicket gate on the right, and follow a footpath to where two† magnificent trees crown the hill; it is wisest to wait until passing along the level ridge,

* The little inn is somewhat romantically styled the 'Golden Grove;' before it is a large tree, the branches of which spread luxuriantly at about eight feet from the ground, and support a railed platform, fitted round the central stem, upon which are a table and seats, embosomed among the leaves and branches, the ascent being by a flight of steps.

† There were originally four; we remember three, but two have been lately destroyed.

you arrive at the 'view point,' and there, spread around you is such a panorama as England only can show, and show against the world for its extreme richness.* On the left is Cooper's Hill, which Denham, that high-priest of 'Local poetry,' long ago made famous ; in the bend just where it meets the plain, you see the towers of Windsor Castle ; there is Harrow Hill, the sun shining brightly on its tall church ; a deep pall hovers over London, but you can see the dome of St. Paul's looming through the mist ; nay, we have heard of those who have told the hour of the day upon its broad-faced clock, with the assistance of a good glass. How beautifully the Thames winds ! Ay ! there is the grand stand at Epsom, and there Twickenhem, delicious soft, balmy Twickenham ; and Richmond Hill—a very queen of beauty !

Yonder, beyond the valley, are Fox's hills crowned with lofty pines—and that is the church at Staines, and as you turn, there again is Cooper's Hill ; Laleham seems spread as a tribute at your feet, and there is no end to the villages and mansions—the parks, and cottages like snow-drops in a parterre, and church spires more than we can number ; while close behind us are the stones, piled thickly one on the other,—the only relics of the holy chapel of St. Anne.†

How grandly the promontory of St. George's Hill stands out—sheltering Weybridge, and forming a beautiful back-ground to Byfleet and the banks

* St. Anne's Hill, anciently called Eldbury or Oldbury Hill, has on its top visible traces of an encampment. There is a group of trees on its summit near which stood a small chapel dedicated to St. Anne, of which a few stones are now all that remains. They are shown in our cut. It is a spot which attracts all lovers of nature by the beauty of the view. Cowley, in a letter dated May 21, 1665, says, 'methinks you and I and the Dean (Dean Spratt) might be very merry upon St. Anne's Hill. You might very conveniently come hither by way of Hampton Town, lying there one night.' A curious instance of the badness of roads and inconvenience of travelling in those days, Hampton being but thirteen miles from London, and Chertsey only twenty.

† In Chertsey Church is a black marble tablet to Laurence Tomson, buried there, and one of the earliest translators of the New Testament into our language, of which two editions were published in the reign of Queen Elizabeth. He resided during the last twenty years of his life at Laleham, and died in 1608. Anthony Wood speaks of his being a great logician and philosopher, and states that a report was then current at Chertsey that he built the house which now stands on the top of St. Anne's Hill, out of the ruins of St. Anne's Chapel, and on the very spot where that chapel stood, having a prospect into several counties ; if so, these stones are, probably, the relics of St. Anne's Chapel and Laurence Tomson's house.

of the Wey ; not forgetting its ruins—a Roman encampment of two thousand years ago, and its modern ornaments of rare trees, of which a generous nobleman* has made common property, to be enjoyed daily by all who choose. At the foot of this richly planted hill, is the beautiful park of Oatlands—on the eve of becoming an assemblage of villa-grounds.

The Nun's Well

How pleasant to feel that we can account, by our own knowledge of that glowing mount—for all the shades formed by the hills and hollows, and different growths of trees in the depths or heights of 'the encampment' which forms the delight of many a toilsome antiquary. Beyond are the more distant eminences of the North Downs, and a tract of country extending into Kent. But we have not yet explored the beauties of this

* The Earl of Ellesmere.

our own hill of Chertsey ; truly, to do so would take a day as long as that of its own black cherry fair.

A path to the left, among the fern and heather, leads to a Well famed for its healing properties—it is called the 'Nun's Well' ;* even now, the

peasants believe that its waters are a cure for diseases of the eye ; the path is steep and dangerous, and it is far pleasanter to walk round the brow of the hill and overlook the dense wood which conceals the well, fringing the meadows of Thorpe, than to seek its tangled hiding-place in the dell. The monks of old would be sorely perplexed if they could arise,

* The spring, called the 'Nun's Well,' once used medicinally, and which rarely freezes, is lined with stone, and is almost hidden by the vegetation which flourishes thickly around it. It is on the north side of the declivity, and on the east is another spring formerly celebrated for its virtues. It is in a wood called 'Monk's Grove.'

to account for the long line of smoke which marks the passage of the different trains along their railroads. But we turn from them to enjoy a ramble round the brow of St. Anne's Hill; the coppice which clothes the descent into the valley, is so thick, that though it is intersected by many paths you might lose yourself half-a-dozen times within an hour; if it be evening, the nightingales in the thickets of Monksgrove have commenced their chorus, and the town of Chertsey, down below, is seen to its full extent, its church tower toned into beauty by the rich light of the setting sun, while through the trees and holly thickets you obtain glimpses of the Guildford and Leatherhead hills, so softly blue, that they meet and mingle with the sky.

Those who feel no interest in monkish chronicles, may reverence St. Anne's Hill, because of its having been the favourite residence of Charles James Fox, the contemporary of Pitt and Burke and Sheridan and Grattan, at a period when men felt strongly and spoke eloquently. The site of the house on the south-eastern side of the hill, is extremely beautiful, and it is much regretted in the neighbourhood that it finds so little favour in the heart of its present noble proprietor. The grounds are laid out with much taste; there is a noble cedar planted by Mrs. Fox, when only the size of a wand. The statesman's widow survived her husband more than thirty-six years, but never outlived her friends or her faculties. There is a temple dedicated to Friendship, which was erected to perpetuate the coming of age of one of the late Lords Holland; on a pedestal ornamented by a vase, are inscribed some verses by General Fitzpatrick; another placed by Mrs. Fox to mark a favourite spot where Mr. Fox loved to muse, is enriched by a quotation from the 'Flower and the Leaf,' concluded by two graceful stanzas—

'Cheerful in this sequester'd bower,
From all the storms of life removed,
Here Fox enjoy'd his evening hour
In converse with the friends he loved.

And here these lines he oft would quote,
Pleased from his favourite poet's lay,
When challenged by the warbler's note
That breathed a song from every spray.'

At the bottom of the garden is a grotto, which must have once possessed many attractions, and above it, there is a pretty little quaint chamber that was used as a tea-room, when, according to the custom of the time, the English drank tea by daylight; it is adorned by painted glass windows; there are portraits of the Prince of Wales, and Mr. Fox, when both were looking their best, and the balcony in front commands a delicious view of the surrounding country.

The Temple of Friendship.

The peasantry are still loud in their praise of 'Madam Fox;' and some remember with gratitude the education they received at her school, and love to tell how the old lady was drawn there at 'feast times,' to see how they all looked in their new dress. She certainly retained her sympathy with the young, and put away the feelings and habits of old age with a determined hand, for, it is said, when she was eighty she took lessons on the harp. The present generation remember personally nothing of the great statesman; he has become history to us, and we must look to history, garbled as it always is, and always will be, by the opinions and feelings of its writers, to determine the position of Charles James Fox in the annals of his country. Those who were admitted to his society have written with enthusiasm of his social qualities, and bestow equal praise on his brilliant talents, his affability of manner, and the generosity of his

disposition. He was the third son of Henry Fox, afterwards Lord Holland, and his mother was the eldest daughter of Charles, second Duke of Richmond, and consequently great-grand-daughter to Charles II.; the maternal descent is one of blotted royalty, of which a man like Fox, could not have been proud. His academic course was unmarked by any of those honours of which Oxford men are so ambitious, and yet, like his great rival, William Pitt, he became a statesman before he was of age.

At St. Anne's Hill he enjoyed as many intervals of repose and tranquillity as could fall to a statesman's lot; in the time of wars and tumults, how he must have luxuriated in its delicious quiet, surrounded by friends who dearly loved him; and swayed only for good by the wife who (although it is known that her early intimacy with him was such as prevented her general recognition in society), according to the evidence of all who knew her, was the minister only to his better thoughts and nobler ambitions, and who weaned him from nearly all the follies and vices which stained his youth and earlier manhood. Various causes led to his death, before age had added infirmities to disease. He died at Chiswick House, and his last words addressed to Mrs. Fox were, 'I die happy.' It is said he wished to be buried at Chertsey, but his remains were interred in Westminster Abbey.

The brilliant Sheridan pronounced so elegant an eulogium on his character, that it is pleasant to think of it in those shades where, as we have said, he so often sought and found repose: 'When Mr. Fox ceased to live, the cause of private honour and friendship lost its highest glory, public liberty its most undaunted champion, and general humanity its most active and ardent assertor. In him was united the most amiable disposition with the most firm and resolute spirit; the mildest manners, with the

most exalted mind. With regard to that great man, it might, indeed, be well said, that in him the bravest heart and most exalted mind sat upon the seat of gentleness.'

There is, at all events, an imaginary pleasure in turning from the wearing-out turmoil of a statesman's life, to what the world believes the tranquil dreams of a poet's existence. But there are few things the worldling so little understands as literary industry, or so little sympathises with as literary care. We have no inclination to over-rate either its toils or its pleasures, and perhaps no life is more abundantly supplied with both. Its toils must be evident to any who have noted the increasing literary labour,

which is necessary to produce the ordinary sources of comforts; but its high and holy enjoyments are not so apparent; they are so different from those of almost all others as not to be easily explained or understood; but above all other gifts, the marvellous gift of poesy is a distinction conferred by the Almighty, and should be acknowledged and treasured as such. We know little of a poet's studies except by their imperishable produce, and it is a common but ill-founded prejudice to imagine regularity or diligence incompatible with high genius. Genius is neither above law, nor opposed to it; but as many have a poetic taste and temperament *without* the inspiration, the world is apt to mistake the eccentricity of the pretender for the outward and visible sign of genius. Whether or not the poet of the Porch-house of Chertsey had the actual poetic fire we do not venture to determine. Abraham Cowley takes a prominent position amongst the poets of our land, and the eventful times in which he lived, and his participation in their tumults give him additional interest in all the relations of his anxious and not over-happy life. It is recorded of him that he became a poet in consequence of reading the Faërie Queene, which chance threw in his way while yet a child. In allusion to this, Dr. Johnson gave his well-known definition of genius—'A mind of large general powers, accidentally determined to some particular direction.' We had almost dared to say this is rather the definition of a philosopher than of one who comprehended the spirituality of a marvellous gift. Abraham Cowley—the posthumous son of a London grocer—owed much to his mother. She, by her exertions, procured him a classical education at Westminster School. She lived to see him loved, honoured, and great, and what was better still, and more uncommon, grateful. At the age of fifteen he published a volume called 'Poetic Blossoms,' which he afterwards described as 'commendable extravagancies in a boy.' He obtained a scholarship in Trinity College, Cambridge, in 1636, and there took his degree; but was ejected by the Parliament, and thence removed to Oxford. Shortly after, he followed the Queen Henrietta to Paris, as Secretary to the Earl of St. Albans, and was employed in the court of the exiles in the most confidential capacity. In 1656 he returned to England, and was immediately arrested as a suspected spy. He submitted quietly—the royalists thought too quietly—to the dominion of the Protector, but his whole life proved that he was no traitor. At the Restoration, that great national disappointment, his claims upon the ungrateful monarch were met by a taunt and a false insinuation—he was told that his pardon was his reward! Wood said 'he lost the place by certain enemies of the Muses;' certain 'friends of the Muses,' however, procured for him the lease of the Porch-house and farm at Chertsey, held under the Queen, and the great desire of his life—solitude—was obtained.

The place still seems a meet dwelling for a poet, and is, perhaps, even more attractive to strangers than St. Anne's Hill. The porch, which caused his residence to be called 'The Porch-house,' was taken down during the last century by the father of its present proprietor, the Rev. John Crosby Clarke, and the house is now known as 'Cowley House.'* It is situated near the bridge, which crosses a narrow and rapid stream, in a lonely part of Guildford Street; a latticed window which overhangs the road is the window of the room in which the Poet expired; on the outside wall Mr. Clarke has recorded his reason for removing the porch. 'The porch of this house, which projected ten feet into the highway, was taken down in the year 1786, for the safety and accommodation of the public.'

'Here the last accents flowed from Cowley's tongue.'

The appearance of the house from Guildford Street, is no index to its size or conveniences.† You enter by a side gate, and the new front of the dwelling is that of a comfortable and gentlemanly home; the old part it is said was built in the reign of James the First, and what remains is sufficiently quaint to bear out the legend; the old and new are much mingled, and the modern part consists of one or two bed-rooms, a large dining-room, and a drawing-room, commanding a delicious garden view, the meanderings of the stream, and a long tract of luxuriant meadows, terminated by the high and richly timbered ground of St. Anne's Hill. A portion of the old stairway is preserved, the wood is not as has been stated oak, but sweet chesnut. One of the rooms is panelled with oak, and Cowley's study is a small closet-like chamber, the window looking towards St. Anne's

* The large outer porch of Cowley's house had chambers above it, and beneath the window in front a tablet was affixed, upon which was inscribed the epitaph 'upon the living author,' which Cowley had written for himself, whilst living in retirement here, commencing

'Hic, O Viator, sub lare parvulo,
Couleius hic est conditus hic jacet.'

It is represented in its original condition in the two views we have engraved.

† Some additional rooms have been added to the house by the same occupant, who has, however, religiously preserved all the old rooms, which still exhibit the 'fittings' that existed in Cowley's time. The bed-chambers are wainscoted with oaken panels. The staircase is a very solid structure, with ornamental balusters, leading toward the small study in which the poet wrote,—a little back room, about five feet wide, looking upon the garden. It may be distinguished in our back view of the house, by a figure placed at the window. Cowley ended his life in this house, at the early age of forty-nine.

Hill.* It is never difficult to imagine a poet in a small chamber, particularly when his mind may imbibe inspiration from so rich and lovely a landscape. Beside the group of trees, beneath whose shadow the poet frequently sat, there is a horse-chesnut of such exceeding size and beauty, that it is worthy a pilgrimage, and no lover of nature could look upon it without mingled feelings of reverence and affection.†

Cowley's Seat.

Here then amid such tranquil scenes, and such placid beauty, the 'melancholy Cowley,' passed the later days of his anxious existence; here we may fancy him receiving Evelyn and Denham, the poets and men of letters of his troubled day, who found the disappointments of courtly life, more than their philosophy could endure. Here, his friendly biographer, Doctor Spratt, cheered his lonely hours.

* The father of the present proprietor was Chamberlain of London, and greatly beloved and respected in Chertsey. It is a happiness to be able to record also how much the Rev. Mr. Clarke deserves the gratitude of the dwellers in our little town. During the late visitation of the cholera, his attention was drawn to the crowded state of the churchyard, and he not only made a grant of a piece of land to the parish as a cemetery, but has been at the sole expense of enclosing it, and erecting the necessary buildings for the purposes of interment.

† There is also in the garden a walnut-tree of which the history is curious. When Mr. Clarke was sheriff of London, it was a custom for the out-going sheriff to present to the in-coming sheriff, when he transferred to his custody the prisoners in Newgate, a bag of walnuts; one of these walnuts Mr. Clarke planted in the garden, of which it is now—more than half a century having passed—the pride.

Cowley was one of those fortunate bards who obtain fame and honour during life. His learning was deep, his reading extensive, his acquaintance with mankind large. 'To him,' says Denham in his famous elegy,—

> 'To him no author was unknown,
> Yet what he wrote was all his own.'

His biographer adds, 'There was nothing affected or singular in his habit, or person, or gesture; *he understood the forms of good breeding enough*

to practice them without burdening himself or others.' This indeed is the perfection of good breeding and good sense.

Having obtained, as we have said, the Porch-house at Chertsey, his mind dwelt with pleasure—a philosophic pleasure—upon the hereafter, which he hoped for in this life of tranquillity, and the silent labour he so dearly loved; but he was destined to prove the reality of his own poesy—

'Oh life, thou *Nothing's* younger brother,
So *like* that one might take one for the other.'

The career of Abraham Cowley was never sullied by vice,* he was loyal without being servile, and at once, modest, independent, and sincere. His character is eloquently drawn by Doctor Spratt. 'He governed his passions with great moderation, his virtues were never troublesome or uneasy to any; whatever he disliked in others he only corrected by the silent reproof of a better practice.'

He died at Chertsey on the 28th of July, 1667,† and was interred in Westminster Abbey; a throng of nobles followed him to his grave, and the worthless king who had deserted him, is reported to have said, that Mr. Cowley had not left a better man behind him in England.

It is said the body of Cowley was removed from Chertsey by water, thus making the Thames he loved so well the high-way to his grave; there is something highly poetic in this idea of a funeral, so still and solemn, with the oars dropping noiselessly in the blue water. Pope in allusion to it says

'What tears the river shed,
When the sad pomp along his banks was led;'

which rather inclines us to the belief, that in this, as in many other instances, the poetic reading is not the true one,—

'The muses oft in lands of vision play:'

but the fact that he died at Chertsey, as much respected as a man, as he was admired as a poet, is certain; and his house is often visited by strangers,

* Brayley in his 'History of Surrey,' states that Cowley accompanied by his friend, Dean Spratt, having been to see a 'friend,' did not set out for his walk home until it was too late, and had drunk so deep, that they both lay out in the fields all night; this gave Cowley the fever that carried him off. Brayley's authority for this slander (which is not borne out by the poet's previous course of life), is 'Spence's Anecdotes.'

† On comparing dates, it is evident that Cowley could not have enjoyed his retirement more than between two and three years.

who are permitted to see his favourite haunts by the kindness of its proprietor, who honours the spot so hallowed by memories of 'the melancholy Cowley;'—he who considered and described 'business' as—

'The contradiction to his fate.'

Thoroughly to appreciate England, the stranger must leave its mighty Babylon;—to understand the rich treasures of her actual beauty, he must

Trees on St. Anne's Hill

quit the iron-shod highways of her traffic, and away, from even her country towns, into her villages; abandon himself, heedless of the passing hours, to the wonderful fertility and loveliness of her bye-lanes, her high and fragrant hedge-rows, her unrivalled parks, timbered with gigantic trees, and clothed in tints of ever-varying underwood. He must sit beneath the shadows of her church steeples, when the bells are ceasing to chime for morning service, and the sons and daughters of the village crowd to render the homage of consecrated prayer to the Almighty: he must inhale the rich perfume of her cottage gardens; he must survey the swelling and folding hills, the placid and fertilising rivers; he must loiter, again and again, in her lanes, creeping close to the hedges to permit the richly-laden wagons to pass on; he must pause beside the entrances of her suburban villas,—and, stranger that he is! wonder at the marvellous order, and regularity, and neatness of every arrangement; seeing that flowers grow, and turf is levelled, and arbours are twined, as they are in no other country of the world: so that hill and dale, wood and park and field, castle and cottage, look one universal garden, where tillage seems as a garlanded pastime, and the wildest luxuriance of nature is tempered—perhaps too much tempered—into beauty.

In Scotland — stern, rigid, right-hearted Scotland — mountains and streams, and lakes, and magnificent rocky passes abound; but there is little richness to repose upon, little that gives assurance of the abounding, overflowing prosperity of England—*too little*, for our taste, of the garden-like aspect, so suggestive of home and home delights. In depopulated Ireland there are the unfilled outlines of everything great and nothing accomplished,—except by nature; the amazing fertility of the soil contrasting painfully with careless farming and ruined 'cabins.' The bewildering beauty of Killarney and the loveliness of the county Wicklow, steep the soul in sadness, because of the misery that clothes a fine cordial-hearted people in rags, and the unfortunate policy which still trails them through the 'Slough of Despond' in which so many have perished: thus our spirits are blighted, and our sense of the beautiful is dulled by sorrow for sufferings we cannot alleviate.

How our English hearts rejoice when we pass the liquid barrier of our sea-girt isle, into the fertile, peaceful, rich, and glowing beauty of dear old England! How do we gladden at the reality of our return HOME! How we joy in the noble trees, the park-like meadows, the delicious lanes and hedge-rows,—the abundance of rural delights, which are fraught with a thousand times the enjoyment we derive from any foreign travel in the 'mere country.'

The overpowering and wonder-working provincial cities of England—filling space with the magnitude of their utilities—afford subject-matter for the philosopher and the 'man of business;' but for ourselves, we love the pastoral employments of England, we shun the power-loom, the railroad, and the steam-engine, and when we desire enjoyment we seek it,

'In cool grot and mossy cell,'

by dimpled brooks, where, through the woodland lacings of the trees, the blue arch of heaven reminds us of a future home, and the sunbeams, as they dapple the rich sward beneath, tell of bright pathways to eternity.

Of late, the world has given itself up, soul and body, as it were, to railway travelling; we cannot project a journey of twenty miles without inquiries as to the 'next station,' and an immediate reference, not to the county map, but the almost unintelligible almanac of the railway, more perplexing in its 'ups' and 'downs' than the most intricate rule in algebra; but which we regard, nevertheless, as an oracle, regulating our movements and our time thereby. We make no appeal from the laws of the steam-king; we relinquish the independence of posting; we are content to stop alike at the most convenient or inconvenient distances from our object, provided we stop at a 'station.' We give our freedom, our comfort, our WILL in all matters of movement to the despot STEAM! We only use our horses to pay visits, and our carriages as make-shifts—'where there is no train!' We submit our motives to the locomotive, and yield us, a willing sacrifice, in helpless listless multitudes, to the wholesale traffickers in steam and iron.

Happily for us, our little innocent railroad terminates, as we have said, peacefully enough at Chertsey; it arrives at its shady terminus in anything but an ostentatious manner, and, to confess a truth, has made our tardy carriers wondrous civil, and reduced the price of coal,—it leaves us plenty of highways and byeways, it has not displaced an inch of the old abbey meadows, or interfered with the sacred groves of St. Anne's Hill. It seems, as we have before said, rather ashamed of disturbing our rural ways at all, seeing it has so very little to do; its puffs are reduced to sighs, and its whole bearing is really so unobtrusive that we scarcely object to its neighbourhood, and if it were drawn by a horse instead of an engine, we believe it might even look in keeping with the crowned head of St. George's Hill, and the mimic pine forest, through which, when detached from its parent train, it creeps along its own particular 'siding' from the Weybridge Station. Leaving it, therefore, in peace, we proceed musingly on this our pilgrimage towards THE DWELLING OF THOMAS DAY.

Thomas Day! the eccentric and accomplished author of 'Sandford and Merton,' the friend of Lovel Edgeworth,—Thomas Day, who planted the dark woods of Anningsley, which sweep round the bend of Timber Hill, skirting the wild village of Brocks, the still wilder common of Woking, and separated only by the hill from the Saxon holding of Ottershaw! We take the lower road of St. Anne's Hill, fringed as it is with laurels and over-hanging shrubs; and ever and anon a peep at a grotto, a temple, or an undulating lawn realises Arcadia. Away rapidly, yet without the assistance of steam, through a road shaded by picturesque trees, and commanding a view of Fox's Hills, until we come to a railing, inclosing a modern Elizabethan cottage, suggestive of far more comfort than belonged to the period. The name—Almner's Barns—reminds us of the appropriation of the estate to the almoners of Chertsey Abbey, becoming in progress of time, vested in the crown at the period of the suppression of religious houses. Tradition says that for a long, long time, this estate was occupied by the Wapshott family, both as tenants to the abbots of Chertsey and to the crown; the same tradition, leaning to the marvellous, declares that these old heritors of the soil had continued to cultivate the same spot of earth from generation to generation, ever since the reign of Alfred, by whom the farm on which they resided was granted to Reginald Wapshott, their ancestor. This is a curious legend in farm history: tradition moreover adds that the ancestor of the Wapshotts was standard-bearer to Alfred, but turned his sword into a ploughshare, and became a farmer. There is, we are told, abundant proof that for at least five hundred years the Wapshotts rented this property, but during the period that the crown estates in Chertsey were held by his late Royal Highness the Duke of York, the rental of Almner's Barns was considerably increased; and, after a heart-breaking struggle to retain the farm of his ancestors, the last of this humble but time-honoured family, resigned what he felt he could not profitably or honestly retain. It is exceedingly interesting to converse with the aged, but clear-headed and firm-hearted man—the representative of the ancient yeoman-farmer race—who still resides in our pensive little town of Chertsey ; he is an admirable specimen of the hale old English farmer, who guided his own plough and gloried in his team. He speaks freely of his long and lost inheritance, and believes that his ancestor was *warrener,* not armour-bearer to Alfred.

He argues 'that none of his descendants were inclined to cultivate the art of war, but that all were peace-loving, industrious farmers, and that if

Kitchen at Almner's Barn

their ancestors had been war-like, the war spirit would have descended to some among them.' At all events, whether the story of the standard be true or not, it is certain that the same family has occupied the same farm for several hundred years—never above, and never below, the rank of yeomen-farmers. Mr. Wapshott told us it was remarkable that his father died the very day they received notice to leave Almner's Barns, 'which,' he added, 'was a most happy change for him, as he continually said the government would never turn the family out :' adding 'but I knew better.' The measure was very unpopular in the neighbourhood, where the Wapshotts were much respected.* England of late has deserted ancestral for mammon worship, but this fine intelligent old man is still a subject of interest and an object of great respect in his native district.

He tells us there has long been a saying in Surrey that no Wapshott was ever very rich or very poor, and that he, the last of his race, will go to the grave in strict fulfilment of the adage. He dwells upon his ancestors' fondness for field sports—it may be they were too fond of them, and maintained large hospitality in a warm country fashion, dining and supping as they did on a long oak table, the servants 'below the salt,' the farmer's family and friends at the upper end, and that concluded, they assembled within the walls of the great chimney which is still, as you see, in a degree preserved at Almner's Barns; and while the mistress and her daughters spun or worked, and the servants were busied according to the season, the song was sung, the story told, and the events of the neighbourhood talked over. We cannot but think it melancholy that these old heritors have passed for ever from their holding; it is the going out of a singular race, the extinguishing of a great fact in rural history; and shining and pleasant as Almner's Barns looks now, and though we wish all good to its present possessor, we regret that it has passed into his hands.

* A newspaper of the period just before the Wapshott's compulsory flitting from their inheritance, gave the following sketch of this 'farming family:'—'In the parish of Thorpe, between Chertsey and Egham, there resides a family, the most ancient perhaps in Europe, though by no means the most conspicuous.

'While disease, the sword, and sometimes the gallows, or the guillotine, have reduced or extinguished so many families, while the revolutions in human affairs have elevated some and sunk others in obscurity, through all the vicissitudes of Church and State, the peaceful family of Wapshott has continued to cultivate the same spot of earth, ever since the time of king Alfred. The storms which swept away such multitudes during the contests of York and Lancaster, passed harmless over this obscure dwelling. The Saxon, Danish, or Norman conquests affected them not, and every king, from Alfred to George III., inclusive, may see the same space of a few acres, freely yielding its produce to the laborious hands of a Wapshott.

'This family never experienced any elevation, and its humility is such as to exempt it from danger of depression. * * * * The pride of ancestry which swells in the bosom of a Courtenay, a Howard, or a Russell, is unknown to the lowly bosom of a Wapshott, whose blood flows on in an uncontaminated stream from the remotest ages:—he tills the same land that was ploughed by his grandfathers, and then sinks into the same grave.

"Doom'd to the spot on which he grew,
He seeks his native bed."'

Leaving Almner's Barns, we turn up 'Hardwick Court Lane,' passing several tangled-looking cottages, and the green where once a fair was held; (after the lapse of twenty years, forgotten! with all its revels, its buying and selling, and cheating and winning, as if it never had been!) this pretty lane brings us out opposite the noble park of Botleys—the finely built and richly wooded seat of Robert Gosling, Esq.—which we skirt, shaded by its umbrageous trees on one side, and those of Bretlands on the other, and leaving the tiny villa of Marylands to the right. On, along this wide and well-kept road, until we arrive at the old Saxon village of Ottershaw; on

—and up Timber Hill, pausing on its summit to inhale the pure fresh breeze, and take in, at a glance, the beauty and variety of the surrounding country. To the left, crouching beneath the shelter of the pine wood, is the lodge and gate of ANNINGSLEY, and the enjoyment of a wild wood drive is indeed refreshing, when, however high and hot the sun, the shadows of those perfumed trees lie closely upon beds of moss and waves of fern and heather.

What a delicious wood it is! wild and wandering—untrimmed and prodigal of its own peculiar beauty; such deep-toned red-brown stems to the lofty firs, whose dark-green spines mat above our heads, where the summer breeze makes such reed-like music that we could fancy it the court of Pan himself. We hear the bleating of the lambs in the far-off meadows, and the soft tinkling of the sheep-bell; the whistle of the blackbird, the loud daring song of the missel-thrush, and the soft whispering 'coo' of the little brown dove,—'Brown Bessy,' as the boys call her. The insect world revel in this shady place,—the stag-beetle and the greedy dragon-fly are of enormous size, and wood-lizards and stony-eyed frogs rove among the moss, while the 'game' rustle about the spiral fern. We remember, last spring, seeing piles of fir-trees—shorn of their boughs—heaped outside the gates, and we trembled lest the wood had been despoiled of its greatest beauty,—'cleared,' or 'trimmed,' or 'untangled,'—but no, the hand of the spoiler had not impaired the character of the dark woods of Anningsley, and the only regret we feel is when they are left behind, and we reach a short tract of cultivated land through which the drive passes to the house.*

The house, we can hardly tell how, looks put away in a corner, though there is no corner to put it in; but it is exactly the sort of house we should have imagined Mr. Day, in his eccentricity, would have desired. Something shy and mysterious, commodious and unpretending; peeping, rather than looking, at the wild, solitary world beyond, and loving uncultivated, rather than cultivated, nature,—even at the time that his fine mind and benevolent heart were acting together for the good of present and future generations.

Some years ago it was our privilege, while visiting Edgeworthstown, to hear much of this singular man, from Maria Edgeworth, who loved to speak of her father's friends. It was pleasant to hear her talk of the author of 'Sandford and Merton,' as she talked of every one, developing a character in a sentence, and touching the foibles of humanity with rays of her own light and good-nature until they almost brightened into perfections. Much of her power and innate cheerfulness she inherited from her father, who, though very different from Mr. Day, was his chosen friend from the time when Mr. Edgeworth was pursuing his mingled path

* At the time when Mr. Day purchased this estate, there were at least 20,000 acres of land lying waste in its immediate vicinity. It lies about three miles south of Chertsey, but the district was as little visited, and the people as ignorant, as if in the wilds of the New Forest. It was among such unpropitious circumstances the philosopher seated himself to improve the soil and its inhabitants.

of philosophy, amusement, and mechanics, at Hare Hatch, where Mr. Day, who then lived with his father and mother at Bear Hill, in Berkshire, called upon him and sought his acquaintance.* 'To the day of his death,' Mr. Edgeworth has written, and the characters are well drawn, 'we continued to live in the most intimate and unvarying friendship,—a

[illegible]

friendship founded upon mutual esteem, between persons of tastes, habits, pursuits, manners, and connections totally opposite. A love of knowledge and a freedom from that admiration of splendour which dazzles and enslaves mankind were the only essential points in which we entirely agreed. Mr. Day was grave, and of a melancholy temperament; I, gay, and full of "constitutional joy." Mr. Day was not a man of strong passions; I was. He delighted, even in the company of women, to descant on the evils brought upon mankind by love; and yet he could not avoid frequently tempting his fate, and what was still more extraordinary, he expected that, with a person neither formed by nature nor cultivated (at that time) by

* Day was born, in 1748, in Wellclose-square, London, and received the first rudiments of his education at the Charter-house, completing his acquirements at Corpus Christi College, Oxford. He studied for the law, and was called to the bar, but the pursuit was ungenial to his tastes, and his fortune being ample, he studied to indulge it by a connection with the first literary men of the day, in whose friendship and correspondence he found the greatest pleasure, and to one of whom—Rousseau—he dedicated his 'Dying Negro.'

art to please, he should win some female wiser than the rest of her sex, who should feel for him the most romantic and everlasting attachment,—a paragon!—who should forget the follies and vanities of her sex for him—who

> "Should go clad like our maidens in grey,
> And live in a cottage on love.'"

Mr. Edgeworth says that Mr. Day's exterior was not prepossessing: 'He seldom combed his raven locks, though he was remarkably fond of washing in the stream.' Gentlemen seldom agree with ladies in their estimates of manly beauty; we think Mr. Day's portrait decidedly handsome, though the want of *self-esteem*, which must have been a prominent organ in Mr. Edgeworth's development, was evidently deficient in that of Mr. Day; he doubted his own success, and consequently did not succeed. His matrimonial views were a strange mingling of sacrifice and selfishness. Mr. Edgeworth states that, 'for an object which should resemble the image of his fancy, he could give up fortune, fame, life,—everything but virtue;' but he expected the lady to do the same, to yield up to his her habits, and even tastes, down to the selection of a glove or a ribbon. Love will do this, and more, spontaneously; but love is impatient of dictation. He attached himself to Mr. Edgeworth's sister, but the lady was not to be entreated, and, after this disappointment—the herald of others—Mr. Day put in practice a scheme which had long occurred to his imagination: he resolved to rear up two girls as equally as possible, under his own eye, hoping they might be friends in childhood, and that before they grew to be women, he might be able to decide which of them would be most agreeable to himself as a wife. The first selected was a beautiful orphan child, from the orphan school at Shrewsbury, whom he called Sabrina Sydney; he then took another from the Foundling Hospital in London, whom he called Lucretia. He first placed these wards at a widow's house, in some court near Chancery Lane, and immediately applied himself to their education. For our own part, we think the plan might have succeeded had they been younger, but they were eleven and twelve years old, and, of course, their feelings and habits were already, in a great degree, formed. His romantic scheme occasioned inquiry and curiosity; to avoid both, he determined to take them to France, where, as they were perfectly unacquainted with the language, their minds would be more under his control. He resided some time at Avignon. Whatever surprise his mode of life or opinions might have excited, his simplicity and purity of conduct, his strict morality, uncommon generosity, and excellent understanding removed. He entertained an unconquerable horror of the empire of fashion over the minds of women: simplicity, perfect innocence, and attachment to himself, were the only qualifications at that time which he seemed to desire in a wife; he was Rousseau-mad, but afterwards recanted the opinions he had endeavoured to practise. After the lapse of a few months, he returned to England and parted with Lucretia, finding her either stupid or unwilling to learn, or unlearn, what he desired. He gave her three or four hundred pounds, placed her under proper protection, and, after a time, she married some small shopkeeper in London.

Every one who knew Mr. Day was desirous of seeing how the second part of this philosophical romance would terminate. Sabrina was most engaging and amiable; her guardian took a pleasant house at Stow Hill, near Lichfield, and steadily pursued his plan. All the ladies of the neighbourhood took notice of the girl, and attributed only the most honourable motives to Mr. Day. There he first met Honora Sneyd, whose personal and mental charms, developed beneath the loving care of the poet, Anna Seward, and her accomplished family, had power to attract the affections of three distinguished men,—Major André, Thomas Day, and Richard Lovell Edgeworth; subsequently Honora became the wife of the latter, but not until after Major André's departure for America, and it is doubtful if she ever responded to the affection which the unfortunate officer felt for her to the last hour of his existence, and which drew forth the beautiful monody on his death from Miss Seward's pen. Sabrina, failing to realise her guardian's dream, he at last placed her at a school: she was wilful, perhaps, touching the colour of a ribbon, or the arranging of her hair, and his feeling towards her fluctuated considerably at last. He provided for her with his usual liberality, and remained her friend until his death.*

* It was singular that when no longer very young, Sabrina was wooed and wed by a barrister, a Mr. Bicknel, who was the companion of Mr. Day when he selected her from among the orphans at Shrewsbury.

Perhaps Mr. Day's new-found love for Honora Sneyd had much to do with his final rejection of Sabrina; he offered this beautiful woman his hand, in a voluminous letter, telling her *honestly* what he expected, which men seldom do until *after* marriage. He was next led captive by the charms of Elizabeth Sneyd, a younger sister of the conquering Honora; but again his want of self-esteem overthrew his wooing; he absolutely went to France, and, in the simplicity and gravity of his heart, determined

('Such is the power of mighty Love')

to cultivate those graces which he despised, in the hope they would aid his course of love.

Mr Edgeworth says, in his Memoirs, 'It was astonishing to behold the energy with which he persevered in these pursuits. I have seen him stand between two boards, which reached higher than his knees, from a desire to make them straight; these boards were adjusted with screws, but the screwing was in vain. I could not help pitying my philosophic friend, pent up in durance vile, for hours together, with his feet in the stocks, a book in his hand, and contempt in his heart.'

And yet, after all this martyrdom, besides 'doing' dancing, and fencing, and riding, on his return he was refused by the fair Elizabeth. Surely any loving, wise woman could have been happy with—and, as the phrase goes, 'managed'—such a man. A man who has sufficient honesty to talk common-sense to a woman before marriage, pays the highest possible compliment to her intellect, and proves that he desires her friendship and companionship as well as her love. Mr. Day talked loudly of man's prerogative; simply because he felt the kindliness of his own nature, he feared he should yield too much, be too heavily bound by the chains he sought. At last, and after, in a right noble-hearted manner, promoting his friend Richard Lovell Edgeworth's marriage with Honora Sneyd, Mr. Day was united to Miss Milnes, of Wakefield, in Yorkshire; a lady of charity and benevolence as unbounded as his own; and the only objection he ever made to this accomplished lady was, that she possessed a large fortune! No wonder that Thomas Day, the author of 'Sandford and Merton,' should be called 'eccentric.'

Maria Edgeworth said Mr. Day 'talked like a book,' and she believed (to use her own expression) 'that he always thought in the same full-dress style.' He wrote as fast as his pen could move; this arose from the early care he had bestowed upon his native language. His poem of the 'Dying Negro' was in advance of our abolition of the slave trade; and it is believed that Dr. Darwin wrote more than one of the stanzas in that touching poem. The history of his authorship of 'Sandford and Merton' was bound up with the Edgeworths.

Mr. Edgeworth and his charming wife, Honora, felt the lack of a particular class of books to follow 'Mrs. Barbauld's Lessons,' and commenced, without any intention of publication, the first part of 'Harry and Lucy, or Practical Education,' as it was called in the title page to the first copies, printed literally for their own children. Mr. Day, much pleased with Mr. Edgeworth's plan, offered to assist him, and, with this intention, began 'Sandford and Merton,' which was first designed as a short story to be inserted in 'Harry and Lucy.'

The illness and death of Mrs. Honora Edgeworth interrupted the progress of the little volume, and Mr. Edgeworth, for a long time, could not endure to think of what her loss had rendered so painful. Meanwhile, Mr. Day wrote on rapidly, and finished, and published, his delightful book. While this floated on the full tide of popularity,—for a period of twenty years, or more,—'Harry and Lucy' remained *perdu* at Edgeworthstown. Miss Edgeworth used to say that all her dear father's literary ambition was for her, and that he at last gave her the first part of 'Harry and Lucy' for a portion of her 'Early Lessons.' Well for the world was it that he did so!

We have heard that Mr. Day underrated 'Sandford and Merton,' and fancied his poems, and some political tracts he wrote, of far higher consequence. But while they are forgotten, the bright story-book of our own childhood will endure; and were it 'got up' in the modern fashion now, and republished, with a few erasures, and the illustrations it so frequently suggests, its popularity would revive, and it would be welcomed wherever the highest and best sentiments of our *moral* nature are cultivated.

It was deeply interesting, while driving through the very wood at Anningsley, which, in 1789, Mr. Day was occupied in planting, to read one of his letters to Mr. Edgeworth, where he confesses, nearly at the commencement, that he is out of pocket 300*l.* a-year by his farm! He says the soil he has taken is barren,—'the most completely barren in England.'—adding, 'I consider the pleasure of everything to lie in the pursuit, and, therefore, while I am contented with the conveniences I enjoy, it is a matter of indifference whether I am five, or twenty years in completing my intended plans. I have, besides, another very material reason, which is that it *enables me to employ the poor.*' This last consideration was ever uppermost in his mind; with all his eccentricity and affected stoicism, his nature was essentially benevolent, brave, and thoroughly independent. While he fancied himself a misanthrope, he was exerting his time and faculties, and expending an ample fortune, for beneficial purposes, relieving, to the utmost of his power, all the wants of his fellow-creatures. Some one has said, that whoever plants a tree is a patriot; although Mr. Day's marriage was unblessed—or unplagued—with children, he delighted in planting those beautiful woods for some future inheritor of the stubborn land.

It may be that our quotations seem somewhat tedious, but we write of one who, in that respect, like his friend Richard Lovell Edgeworth was singularly in advance of his period; in our childhood we revered the author of 'Sandford and Merton' next to the author of 'Early Lessons,' and now never pass beneath the trees he planted without the memory of old feelings creeping into our very heart. Among many blessings we thank GOD that he keeps our 'memory green,' and that our enthusiasm is as genuine as when we first trembled with reverence in the presence of some of those great thinkers whom we hope to meet HEREAFTER. Anningsley, with its varied shadows and mysterious woods, is to us a place of deep interest. Though it is difficult to identify the rooms which were, or were not, occupied by Mr. and Mrs. Day, the house and land have not departed from the family.* The joyful voices of happy children echo through the woods, and tempt one almost to forget that on the confines of that very wood the author and philosopher breathed his last, on the 28th of September, 1789. His death is but another lesson of the uncertainty of

* The present owner of Anningsley is the Hon. James Norton, in right of his wife the grand-niece of Mr. Day.

life, which we too often calculate on, as if it were eternity. Mr. Day held a theory that whenever horses were vicious or unruly, it was simply because they had been harshly treated. Having reared a favourite foal, he determined to 'break it' himself; he mounted the colt, but his horsemanship was not sufficiently good to enable him to keep his seat, when the animal plunged, and eventually threw him, and struck him with his heels so severe a blow on his head that it terminated his existence.*

Mrs. Day was inconsolable; she loved her husband with all the enthusiasm of young romance; never was there a more devoted wife. She loved sufficiently to forget his peculiarities in her admiration of his virtues, and she placed the following epitaph over his remains, in Hargrave Church, Berkshire. The epitaph had been written by Mr. Day for the monument of a friend, but it was well applied to himself:—

'Beyond the reach of time, or fortune's power,
Remain cold stone, remain, and mark the hour,
When all the noblest gifts which heaven ere gave,
Were centred in a dark untimely grave!
Oh! taught on Reason's boldest wings to rise
And catch each glimmering of the open skies!
Oh gentle bosom! oh unsullied mind!
Oh, friend of truth, to virtue, to mankind!
Thy dear remains we trust to this sad shrine,
Secure to feel no second loss like thine.'

The walk from Chertsey to WEYBRIDGE is as pleasant a walk as can be desired; especially on a morning of May, when the weather is cool, and the sun is playing at bo-peep through the fleecy clouds, which yield shade and refreshment to the teeming earth. Those who have no desire to pass through the pretty scattered village of Addlestone (where, here and there, an ambitious 'villa residence' intimates that Londoners are appreciating its salubrity and convenience) may still desire to prolong their walk by rendering homage to the CROUCH OAK, one of the most superb trees in England, which deserves a pilgrimage to its leafy shrine from any genuine

* The accident was the more sad, as it occurred when Mr. Day was paying an affectionate duty which he never omitted, once a year—a visit to his aged mother. She resided at Bear Hill, near Wargrave, in Berkshire, and he was on his journey thither when his horse threw him, and he died on the spot.

lover of nature.* But if this has been already seen, it is pleasanter to wander up Woburn Hill than to pass over the Addlestone railway. The hill is deliciously sheltered from wind, and rain, and heat, by the outspreading foliage of the beautiful trees of Woburn (the seat of the

The Crouch Oak.

Hon. Locke King): and the public road, after crossing Fordwater Bridge, continues between the trickling Bourne and the Basingstoke canal, until it crosses the bridge where the Wey (dividing the parishes of Weybridge and Chertsey), the canal, and the Bourne, unite in one considerable body of water.

* In Brayley's excellent 'History of Surrey,' we are told that 'tradition states that this oak, in former ages, was considered to mark the boundary of Windsor Forest in this direction, and Queen Elizabeth is said to have dined beneath its shadow.' Its girth at 2 feet from the ground is 24 feet. At the height of 9 feet, the principal branch, in itself as large as a tree, shoots out almost horizontally from the trunk to the distance of 48 feet, and is known to have been 8 or 10 feet longer about twenty years ago. Before the enclosure of the manor of Chertsey-Beomond in 1808, this oak stood on the open common; but the plot of ground on which it stands was patriotically purchased by Captain De Visme—who has laid the neighbourhood under an obligation by adding it to his estate, as its former owner had determined to *cut it down!*—and if this had not been done, its decay would have been accelerated by a superstitious practice—namely, that of having the bark peeled off by ignorant females, from an opinion that, taken internally, it operates as a love charm! The name of *crouch* oak may possibly have been given to this tree from the low, crouching form of its chief branches. There is also a tradition that Wickliffe preached under it.

We are told that some rare aquatic plants border the meandering Bourne, and render a stroll along its banks a rich treat to the botanist. The entrance to the village of Weybridge has something of a foreign aspect, owing, perhaps, to its lofty trees and an uninterrupted avenue of limes, between quaint houses that are dimly seen beyond their walled-in gardens. But there are two roads, which, as it were, gird the village and spread out in different directions; one leading to the common and station,

The Wey Bridge.

passes the chapel where the remains of Louis Philippe are for the present interred, and which is rendered still more sacred by the sorrows and tears of a royal, but exiled, family, living not far off—at Claremont—and those of many illustrious pilgrims from their native land. The chapel commands a beautiful view over the breezy heath, bounded by the bold headland of St. George's Hill. We were courteously admitted beneath a domed porch (where the turning of a wheeled gate rings a soft-sounding bell), and conducted through a picturesque and exquisitely-kept garden to the little chapel where the exiled family of France frequently assemble. We then descended to the crypt, containing two tombs—that of the founder of the chapel, a devout man (according to his faith), and that of the first King of the French, who maintained peace in France for eighteen years, and preferred the abdication of his Throne to the shedding of his people's blood.* There was an earnestness and fulness of sorrow within that crypt, which we have not often felt in the midst of elaborate tombs and the pomp and pageantry of death. The perfect and entire silence—the loneliness of the situation—the rays of light pouring directly through the windows upon the founder's tomb, while that of the KING occupied what may be called the centre of the crypt, elevated two steps above the floor, and reaching to the far end of the vault. There is something inexpressibly grand in the simplicity of this last refuge of a

Tomb of Louis Philippe.

great man and a mighty monarch. Our hearts were filled with memories of the past; when we saw him in the radiance of his power—the venerated Ruler of a nation—combining the holiest virtues of domestic life with the dignity and duties of his high position. We remembered his vicissitudes—his large attainments—his suavity and royal bearing—

'All crushed into that small and silent tomb.'

* The chapel is a very small building capable of giving accommodation to fifty persons only; its ground-plan is, however, cruciform.

Great he was in adversity, and great in prosperity: for he had learned the 'uses' of both. Hereafter, he will receive gratitude from France, and justice from History. In him the Arts of Peace had their patron and protector: his choicest rewards were accorded to men of genius: his recognition of *mind* was ever ready and cordial: and to have been useful to his country—or to any country—was the surest road to those public honours of which he was the wise and liberal distributor.

It is, therefore, a privilege to render homage at the grave of the illustrious exile: for it is homage less to the greatness of the monarch than to the virtues of the man!

A crown and sceptre are carved at the head and these few words:—

DEPOSITÆ JACENT
SUB HOC LAPIDE
DONEC IN PATRIAM
AVITOS INTER CINERES
DEO ADJUVANTE TRANSFERANTUR RELLIQUIÆ
LUDOVICI PHILIPPI
PRIMI FRANCORUM REGIS
CLARMONTII IN BRITANNIÆ
DEFUNCTI DIE AUGUSTI XXVI.
ANNO DOMINI MDCCCL.
ÆTAT. LXXVI.

REQUIESCAT IN PACE.*

Upon the steps were placed several garlands, such as decorate the tombs in Père-la-Chaise, and two vases of flowers.† 'These,' said the attendant, 'were placed here by the Queen.' A robin poured forth its wealth of song close to the window. A saintly requiem could not have moved us more; it was so wild and tender—such clear, gushing music; there was no other sound upon the clear, frosty air. We did not move until the chaunt was finished. We ascended into the outer world, and heard the key turned upon the door of that lonely crypt.

The other road, after passing the new church, leads beneath the lime

* Under this stone lie buried the remains of Louis Philippe, first King of the French; until, by God's assistance, they may be transferred into his country, among the ashes of his ancestors. He died at Claremont, in Great Britain, on the 26th of August, 1850, in the 76th year of his age.—May he rest in peace.

† Wreaths of *immortels* are placed in front, upon which we noticed two inscriptions formed in dark flowers—'Regrets Eternels,' 'Au meilleur des Rois,' and the dates '1847—1851.'

avenue more directly to the most interesting part of Weybridge—the entrance to Oatlands Park. The manor of Weybridge anciently belonged to the Abbey of Chertsey ; Henry VIII. obtained possession of Oatlands, and Queen Elizabeth is said to have shot with a cross-bow 'in the paddock.' Anne of Denmark, the wife of James I., took to cultivate silk-worms at Oatlands, and had there a silk-worm room. The youngest son of Charles I. was born there, and was hence styled Henry of Oatlands ; it had previously been settled by the unfortunate Charles, as a dower-land, on Henrietta Maria. The house and domain were much injured during the interregnum, but, after the Restoration, it was returned to the queen in its dilapidated and dismantled state. It has confessed to many masters, and amongst others, to the Earl of Lincoln, who formed the gardens at Oatlands.*

The first gateway leads from the park to Walton-on-Thames ; another, designed by Inigo Jones, and which formed an entrance to the terrace, was not long ago sold for 10*l.*, pulled down, and removed. It was a fine work, and a real loss to the place. The Duke of Newcastle built the far-famed grotto within the park, and after the park and grotto† became the property of the Duke of York, the duchess indulged her feeling and her fancy by the erection of some sixty monuments to the memory of her dogs.

* There is a curious bird's-eye view of the old palace at Oatlands, as it appeared about the time of Elizabeth, in Manning and Bray's 'Surrey,' and which is reproduced on a smaller scale in Brayley's County History. Many of its features closely resemble Hampton Court, particularly its square gate-towers, flanked by octangular turrets. The buildings were exceedingly irregular, the entrance-court a waste walled space of great size, with stabling and offices on each side, a central path leading to the principal gateway, through which a square enclosed court of an oblong form was reached, surrounded with dwellings ; beyond this, another gate, of very similar construction, led to some smaller courts, and a confused triangular assemblage of buildings, seemingly constructed in 'most admired disorder,' with characteristic turrets and gables. The garden wall still exhibits traces of the old palace, in a brick gateway, evidently of the time of Henry VIII., and some remains of vaulted cellars are preserved in other parts of the grounds.

† The grotto is reported to have been constructed by a father and his two sons, who were occupied many years in its formation, at a cost to the Duke of Newcastle of about 40,000*l.* It is entirely composed of minute pieces of spar, coral rock, minerals, and shells, and consists of various apartments and winding passages. The upper room has a domed roof, from which hang stalactites of satin spar, and here George IV., when Prince of Wales, gave one of his luxurious *petits soupers* to a select party of his friends. It was also a favourite retiring-room of the Duchess of York, and the Chinese chairs and other furniture remaining are those she used, the cushions being covered with her needlework.

These are placed at intervals round what was once an ornamental piece of water, stored with gold and silver fish. But her grace's love of the animal creation was only one of the phases of her benevolence; she was a singularly amiable and kind-hearted princess, and there are those in Weybridge, to this day, who speak of her charities with intense gratitude. It was deemed necessary, by some, to erect a monument to her memory, and those who designed to do honour to her excellent qualities also desired to be as sparing as possible of their pecuniary resources. In times long past the column which was known as the 'Seven Dials' in London had been removed, and conveyed, for some forgotten purpose, to a place in our neighbourhood, called 'Sayes Court,'—a handsome, well-wooded residence, whose gables and chimneys form a picturesque object from Crockford Bridge, which spans the stream of the Bourne, on the New Haw and Pyrford roads,—there it lay, for many years, amongst the *débris* of long grass and architectural fragments, and from thence it was again removed and set up at Weybridge; the original direction as to the locality of the Seven Dials* being cast away where it still is, close to a

Column at Weybridge.

* The stone, although marking the '*Seven* Dials,' is hexagonal; and it is clear that it must have been originally cut with six sides only. Indeed, it is recorded that one of the dials served for two streets, opening into one angle. The marks are plainly discernible where the indexes of the various dials were placed, and portions of the metal with which they were secured is still remaining.

public house on the green, and the graduated spire crowned by a coronet, while an inscription is introduced upon the pedestal, expressive of an admiration which deserved a better monument.*

Oatlands Park is, however, *now* only 'Oatlands Park' by courtesy; its glory has departed, and it has been let in lots for building. Its noble trees are removed or retained at the pleasure of those who erect Swiss cottages, or trim bright, glazy villas, amid the silent groves, where once the deer browsed, and the squirrel played, and which often echoed the hunting-horn of royalty. The views over the valley of the Thames are most beautiful, and Windsor Castle towers in the distance. There are many trees, vistas, and glimpses of scenery which still delight the lover of nature, but the once great palace is now park-less, and we cannot but regret that, however desirable for 'building ground,' such a noble heritage should be 'lotted' and cut up for mere utility; it is one of the signs—alas, too many!—that the *poetry* of life is fast fading from among us.

The ascent to St. George's Hill, from either gate, is sufficiently easy for man or horse. The view, from the 'view point,' is more extensive on one side than from its neighbouring hill of St. Anne's; its sides are more precipitous, it is altogether grander and bolder; it stands proudly above the landscape, as if conscious of its Roman encampment,† of its woods,

* A new church has lately been erected at Weybridge, and when a spire is added thereunto, it will be handsome both inside and out. But here Chantrey's monument to the excellent Duchess is thrust into a corner, with all the other tablets and monuments removed from the old church—much to the disgust of all who conceive that God's temple ought to be adorned by the beautiful works of men's hands.

† Though constantly described as a Roman camp, and even sometimes called 'Cæsar's camp,' the irregularity of its form would lead the judicious antiquary to give it an earlier date, and ascribe it to a British origin. Brayley considers it 'one of those hill fastnesses from which our rude ancestors were driven by the superior discipline and weapons of the Roman soldiers.' The discovery of some ancient urns at Silvermere (at the foot of the hill) a few years ago, may be referred to as corroborative of this opinion. These urns were discovered in a grave-mound, and were of unbaked clay, ornamented with a double zig-zag round the rim, and are decidedly of British manufacture. The area of the camp encloses nearly 14 acres of ground; the vallum and ditches are perfectly distinct, the latter very deep in many places. The ground-plan is exceedingly irregular, taking in the crest of the hill, and on the south side is an embankment enclosing the declivity, as if the original camp had been thus added to, or strengthened. On St. Anne's Hill are traces of similar entrenchments, which were, no doubt, formed by the early inhabitants of the country, who would

enriched of late by so many rare trees, of its historic and antiquarian importance; it hardly bends its leafy crown to imperial Windsor; it commands a grand view of the Surrey hills, and mingles Alpine and English scenery together; it is delicious to inhale the breeze, so fresh and pure, that rushes over the valley; and pleasant to rest, after the fatigue of the ascent, on the seats so kindly set apart and sheltered from the sun, by the considerate liberality of its noble proprietor, the Earl of Ellesmere; it was also pleasant, during the feverish summer of 1851, to show the foreigner such a view, so rich in English beauty, and to hear his exclamations of delight and astonishment.

WALTON is another village, quite within a walk of CHERTSEY, even if you skirt the Thames from Weybridge, and leave Oatlands to the right; you then obtain a better view of the double bridge of Walton, and see to advantage the sweep of Lord Tankerville's villa. Walton is a pleasant village to live in, and, having a station of its own, and being near the Thames, it has many summer attractions for those whose duties limit them to a 'convenient distance' from London.

Its church * contains several interesting monuments, and the intelligent clerk, who is not a little proud of the structure, turns up a piece of matting, and shows the flat, grey stone, inscribed to the memory of the once famous astrologer, Lilly, who resided five-and-forty years in Walton; † but the leading attraction of Walton Church is the monument executed by Roubiliac, by order of Grace, Countess of Middlesex, to the memory of her father, the Lord Viscount Shannon, commander of the forces in Ireland.‡

naturally choose such commanding and elevated situations for their fortresses. Coway Stakes is about a mile and a half distant from St. George's Hill, and here Camden and other writers affirm that Cæsar crossed the Thames in pursuit of Cassivellaunus.

* The church is a very ancient structure; it consists of a nave and side aisles, with a chancel beyond. Four pointed arches spring from massive columns on each side of the nave, which were probably constructed in the twelfth century; but the church has undergone so many changes, that its other antique features are lost, or masked by more modern work.

† The stone has been removed from its proper place, over the grave of Lilly, which was on the left side of the communion table. It was placed there by his friend, the visionary antiquary, Elias Ashmole, who records that this 'fair black marble stone' cost him *6l. 4s. 6d.*

‡ He was nephew to the famous Robert Boyle, and "volunteer when a youth at the battle of the Boyne."

Those who remember the doings in England during the Commonwealth may people the churchyard of Walton with a singular assembly when, a few Sundays after the execution of Charles I., a soldier bearing a lighted candle in his hand, having failed to compel the rector of Walton to resign his pulpit to him, mounted a tombstone, and preached one of those extraordinary discourses, so common in that wonder-working age.

We read the other day of a Tuscan city, where every house in which a remarkable person had been born was marked by an inscription: we

[illegible]

render genius no such homage here. A man of singular wit, talent, and learning, Doctor Maginn, died and was buried at Walton, little more than ten years ago. There is no stone inscribed with his name; and we wandered over many half-obliterated mounds before even the sexton could point out to us the spot where he had been dropped into his grave—*

'Alas, poor Yorick!'

There are some curious monuments within the church, and five brasses

* We have also sought in vain for the house in which Admiral Rodney was born, though it is known he was born at Walton.

in memory of a certain John Selwyn, one of himself, another of his wife; one where, mounted on the back of a stag, he is in the act of stabbing it in the throat, and another of no less than 'eleven branches,' all belonging to the said John Selwyn, a forester of Oatlands in the reign of Queen Elizabeth, famous for his deeds of daring; the fifth contains the inscription to their memories.* This parish is also endowed with an instrument for the control of female eloquence, which would in no degree receive homage from the 'Bloomers' of the present day. It is of curious

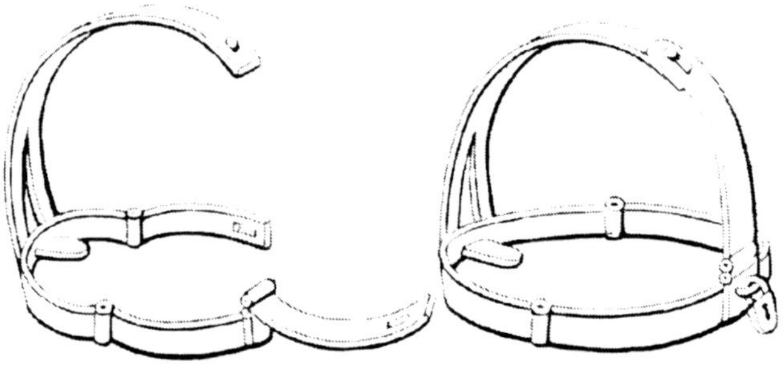

The Scold's Bridle

construction, and, when fixed on, one part enters the mouth, and prevents articulation. It originally bore the following inscription, and the date 1633, but only faint traces now remain of either.

'Chester presents Walton with a bridle,
To curb women's tongues that talk too idle.' †

* These five plates are evidently a series, forming only one memorial to Selwyn and his family, and originally inserted in a grave-stone. The most curious plate is that representing Selwyn stabbing the stag, and it is still more remarkable as it is a *palimpsest* (or brass engraved on both sides), with some variations of the same incident, which has been explained as being, probably, an incorrect version of the exploit, turned face downward, and a more correct one done on the same plate, to save expense. Selwyn was under-keeper of the park at Oatlands in the reign of Elizabeth, and was remarkable for his skill in horsemanship; upon one occasion, during the heat of the chase, he leaped from his horse upon the back of the stag, and, keeping his seat gracefully, notwithstanding all efforts of the affrighted beast, guided it towards the Queen, and drawing his *couteau de chasse*, plunged it in its throat, and it fell dead at her feet.

† It is said that this bridle was presented by the individual whose name it bears because he had lost an estate 'through the instrumentality of a gossiping, lying woman.' Its construction and mode of fastening is shown in our cuts, which exhibit the bridle unfastened, and as it would appear when closed over the head; when locked a flat piece of iron projects

Ashley Park, seated with so much dignity upon its stately lawn, commands the admiration of all wayfarers, and *is said* to have been inhabited by Oliver Cromwell. But the most interesting relic of *his* times is the house of the President Bradshaw. Its effect is much injured by a

[illegible]

narrow street of small houses, built in such a way as effectually to prevent the whole from being seen at once.* The house within is divided and subdivided into small tenements, where old and young are mingled together,

into the mouth, and effectually keeps down the tongue, a triangular opening in the bar above admits the nose, and allows the machine to fit tightly on the head. One of a precisely similar kind is described by Brand in his 'History of Newcastle-upon-Tyne,' and Dr. Plott engraves another in his 'History of Staffordshire,' 'which being put upon the offender,' he tells us, 'by order of the magistrate, and fastened with a padlock behind, she is led round the town by an officer, to her shame, nor is it taken off till after the party begins to show all external signs imaginable of humiliation and amendment.' The town council of Lichfield still possesses one of these bridles, another is at Beaudesert, the seat of the Marquis of Anglesey; but the most curious is at Harnstall Ridware, in Staffordshire, which has apertures for the eyes and nose, giving the face a grotesque appearance, and towering above it like the cap of a grenadier.

* There is a very good engraving of the exterior of this house before the street was built, in Brayley's 'Surrey.' It was then an exceedingly picturesque object. The best notion of its original appearance may be obtained from an examination of the room we engrave, which is now the only unspoilt portion of this once important and interesting house.

as in one large family; one aged woman, who stood in the middle of the room on the ground floor, which exhibits the most considerable remains of the original fittings-up in its carved chimney-piece, panelled wainscoting and strong beams, said 'it was a great house once, but full of wickedness, and no wonder the spirits of its inhabitants troubled the earth to this day,' but all others were silent as to sights or sounds belonging to the world of shadows. Many, doubtless, were the consultations held within these mouldering walls, touching the fate of England, and it is not a matter of wonder that the superstitious who are in its immediate neighbourhood should sometimes there 'see visions and dream dreams.'*

These 'visions and 'dreams' are, of course, less frequent, now that the house of the Regicide is, as it were, 'shored up' by streets, where a ghost of any respectability would find it impossible to wander, even on the darkest night. In old times, the 'good old times,' the house must have been isolated, and far away from any dwelling of equal size or pretension; it was surrounded by a garden, and there is a rumour of a subterranean passage, leading, one report says, to the Thames, another states to the palace at Oatlands, another to Ashley Park. In old times (whether deserving the epithet of 'good' or not is a question), these underground passages and caves were necessary alike for the preservation of property and life, and we believe there are still numerous excavations immediately round our old mansions, which have been either intentionally walled in, or have become choked up by the *débris* of time; it is somewhat remarkable, that, even when discovered and inspected, so little traces have been found of those who sought protection and shelter within their gloomy sanctuary. It is trite enough to say what tales their walls could tell, but it is impossible to look into them without wishing 'these walls had tongues.'

Pyrford is certainly a good long walk from Chertsey, and is, unfortunately for the lovers of the picturesque, but little known. It cannot be called a hamlet, there are too few houses, and neighbourhood it has none. The walk moreover is flat and lonely. We pass through Addlestone, over Crockford or Crokford bridge, then over the canal bridge, and under that

* Tradition affirms that in this house was signed the death-warrant of the unhappy King Charles I.

of the South Western Railway. The country is rough and wild; gravel pits, whose sides are wreathed with fern and heather, patches of fir plantation, with here and there a farm-house swarming with black pigs, lowing calves, and noisy poultry; a cottage half hidden by its abundant orchard; more heather, more fir plantation, more black pigs and poultry, and the roads mottled by the restless shadows of the waving birch trees, whose branches hang with pensile grace, above the hedge rows: as we draw nearer to our destination the trees and hedges mingle, forming a bower above our heads.

'And what was Pyrford, or Piford, or Pyreford?' Truly it has its histories! Of old, old, it belonged to the Abbey of Westminster, then to the Abbey of Sheen, then Elizabeth reclaimed it for the crown, then Edward Lord Lincoln, Lord high Admiral of England at that time, built himself a fair house at 'Pyriford,' but after all this expenditure it would seem as though he had only a life interest in the place, for we find Elizabeth visiting 'John Wolley,' at 'Pirford,' the same 'John Wolley' who succeeded the learned Roger Ascham as her Majesty's Latin secretary; in the eventful course of years it had many masters whose names only live in church books, upon old tombstones, or in forgotten county histories. Evelyn in his Diary speaks of Mr. Denzil Onslow's seat at 'Purford;' and Aubrey calls it a delightful place, 'three miles about,' and tells us how it 'is a fair house standing near the river Wey, and that from the lodge you may overlook the ruins of Newark Abbey, the seven streams running by it, and the rich meadows, watered by them.' He tells of avenues of elms and birches, of a decoy pool, 'with four tunnels,' of the great lake of Sheerwater, 'two miles about.' Alas! all these are gone! the house has been pulled down, the decoy suffered to go to ruin, the lake drained and filled up, population (thin as it seems), and cultivation have overspread the solitude of conservatism, and though the present 'Ladie farm' looks perfectly innocent of aristocratic associations, crouching amid evergreens and roses, its ample byre filled with the

'Lowing herd,'

yet many a

'Yeoman and bowman bold,'

have claimed hospitality, and received a welcome on the self-same spot.

Yes, there is Pyrford Church, or, as we believe it is more correct to call it, chapel. Ascending the path which leads to its humble gate, you pass the pretty little school (unless you like to tarry and hear the pleasant music of young voices), and the gate which leads to the Vicarage, and you exclaim 'What a fine old yew tree!' You are interested by the number of 'green graves,' purely, brightly green, where the grasshopper hops and the white moth glistens in the sunbeam. The church is very small and very old. There is nothing to 'notice' in the interior; the pews of oak,

irregularly placed generally, are old and worm-eaten. The building simply consists of a nave and chancel, with a low tower, surmounted by an ordinary spire rising from the roof of the former. What a primitive-looking old church it is! it belongs so entirely to the past, that you wonder how it has been preserved; and that rude old spire seems so perishing; you look from the Porch, through the trees across to the Vicarage. What a lovely spot, the spot of all others suited for the residence of a country clergyman; and, happily, a good man is there!

You gaze upon it with delight, and think the report of the beauty of Pyrford no exaggeration, but you are only on the threshold of its beauty. Move slowly, and carefully through the long grass—carefully! lest you tread upon those nameless but hallowed graves; you now know, that the withered-looking little church stands upon a commanding mount. You can hardly believe that such is the case—the ascent has been so gradual; now you are close to the hollow tree that for ages has sentinelled the pathway-pass to the rich valley outspread at your feet—THERE! Look at it with loving eyes, where it reposes in the sunshine, while a soft warm mist half shrouds the distant hills, and seems to unite them to the heavens; they are not so grand or so harsh as mountains. Oh, no! our Surrey Hills pretend to nothing so ambitious or so cold; but we are very grateful to them for giving what we so often want—a background to our pictures. To the left are the ruins of Newark Abbey, which the artist would clothe with ivy—though, perhaps, grim and grey as they are, they contrast better with the deep bright green by which they are surrounded.* We will not believe that in old times monks blessed with such a residence ever disturbed the peace of the fair nuns of Ockham:† there is a wicked old ballad which prates of this, but it is doubtless a fable; these however are the ruins, which with their surrounding scenery, composed of rivers and rivulets, foot-bridge and fords, plashy pools and fringed tangled hollows,

* The old Priory of Newark was inhabited by canons regular of the order of St. Augustine, and was founded about the time of Richard Cœur de Lion, by Ruald de Calva, and his wife, Beatrice de Sandes. The church was dedicated to the Blessed Virgin and St. Thomas of Canterbury, and was well endowed with lands by himself and successors; the canons gradually increasing in wealth, and lands, and privileges, until the time of Henry VIII., when it was surrendered to the rapacity of that sovereign by the principal, Richard Lyppescomb, who gained thereby a pension of 40*l.*, and grants to seven other canons belonging to the foundation. The priory church is now so much ruined, that scarcely any of the facing stones remain; the walls are about three feet thick, and exhibit little more than the core of flint, cemented with grout and rubble; the country folks and road contractors formerly came here as to a stone quarry for materials to repair walls and roads, and the wonder is that anything remains of this once important edifice.

† At Ockham, in the adjoining parish, was a nunnery, and the tradition goes that a communication between that building and Newark Abbey was formed by a subterranean passage, which passed beneath the river. It is needless to call attention to the fact, which must have fallen under the observation of all who investigate old buildings, of the frequency with which such tales of subterranean passages are narrated, and their general absurdity.

trees in groups or alone, cattle—enjoying the freshness and food of this happy valley, or gathering round the wide-spreading trees, chewing their cud or tossing their tails at the intruding flies, while there the beauty of the herd remains perfectly motionless, as if conscious of her importance in so lovely a landscape. These, and a hundred other pleasant things—the floating of the rooks beneath the fleecy clouds, the cooing of the ringdoves

Ruins of Newark Priory

in the nearest copse, the impassioned song of the wondrous nightingale from a bough somewhere in the verdant ravine; the coming and going effects of the shadows, now deepening the tone of a clump of hawthorn in the foreground almost into blackness, then spangling the meadow with diamonds; now flying over hill and valley, then lingering on the ruins until they seem steeped in some dark dream of the past; while all the time the purring river keeps circling in little eddies round the supports of the foot-bridge, and taking frothy leaps over huge stones which make-believe to intercept its course from that cavern of foliage from whence it issues to fertilise the meadows of Newark Abbey! Ay, look, and look again, enjoy it ALL—for it is a blessed enjoyment, one forbidden by no law, moral or divine—to enjoy the loveliness of wood and water, hill and dale, with which the Almighty has decked as with a garland our blessed English land. But your pleasant task is not ended until you descend the ravine and reach the foot-bridge; then look up at the old church, and if you have pencil and paper, and do not sketch it on the instant, you will never be an artist!

Between this lovely spot and Woking, somewhere near the healthy, heathy common which bears the same name, once stood the mansion of Sir Edward Zouch, and there it has been written, he often received the visits of of his patron James I. The king went thither from his palace of Oatlands, and according to Mr. Manning a tradition prevails that a turret, still existing on a hill to the north of the house, was built for the purpose of exhibiting a light, as a beacon for the guidance of messengers who resorted to the king at night. We could gossip through a goodly quarto did we speak of all the places deserving remark in our neighbourhood, but one other has an especial interest for us, and we at least found it worthy a visit, though it lies quite away from the very pretty village which bears its name—we mean Byfleet Park. Byfleet* is an admirable village for the artist—a treasure house of long barns, whose roofs are overgrown with moss—its dwellings so well cared for, half farm half cottage houses, its trees so nobly grown, and more than one or two stately venerable mansions opened upon by solid gateways, and protected by massive railings, or walls covered with ivy—it lies low certainly, but that makes vegetation more luxuriant—and what more beautiful to gaze upon than the green ravines

* About the middle of the last century the rectory of Byfleet was held by the Rev. Stephen Duck, who was originally an agricultural labourer, but his poetic talents attracted the notice of Caroline, consort of George II., and though his poetry is forgotten, it procured him the notice and education which led to the living of Byfleet; not long did he enjoy it, for in a fit of melancholy insanity he drowned himself at Reading. There is another instance of elevated circumstances near this, but with a happier result. When the house of James Kirkpatrick Escott, Esq., at Ongar Hill, was building, Sir George Soane worked at its walls, as a brick-layer's boy. There is a monument in Byfleet church to the memory of the amiable and accomplished Joseph Spence.

and bold promontory of St. George's Hill. But the road to Byfleet Park—(a royal chase until purchased from the crown by the late Lord King—) is narrow passing the entrance to the mill, where the Wey dividing its waters circles round an island, which we are told is the very paradise of

Entrance Gate, Byfleet

gardens ; then forward—ploughed land on one side, and on the other the Wey, now broad, now narrow, seen through the copse, and, glancing beneath the tall trees, it shines in the sun like liquid silver, lovely, capricious river that it is ! seldom retaining the same aspect or breadth for half a mile.

The house, as you approach it, has a singularly lonely and deserted appearance; standing so straight and narrow against the clear sky, it looks like something left as a monument of the past: two piers of carved stones are flanked by high walls, and the hall door is reached by a flight of high narrow stone steps, divided and time-worn; it has been for some time used as a farm-house, or rather occupied by the person to whom a portion of what was so long royal property has been let by its present 'lord and master,' the Hon. Locke King, M.P.

The kind courtesy of its occupant permitted us to enter, and the cold lonely aspect of the house was at once changed to one capable of every comfort. Above the fire-place, in the entrance hall, is a coat of arms; but the staircase has been barbarously painted over, though evidently of oak; the rooms are panelled, and 'beautified' (?) by paint, they are lofty and cheerful; the walls are thick, and as the roof has no gutters, the dryness of the house is a proof of its solidity; in one of the bedrooms, a beautifully carved slab of stone-work forms the front of the chimney-piece, and the walls of a little attic which commands a delicious view of the windings of the Wey, and St. George's Hill, was once richly panelled and gilt, but the taste of the times has incrusted it with white-wash; our fair guide disclaimed any act or part in this tragedy, which she assured us was perpetrated before her husband became tenant of the farm.

A portion of these walls, it is believed, heard the stormy wailings of Henry VIII., when the huge baby was (so runs the legend) sent to nurse at Byfleet Park. They have been 'modernised,' the greater part rebuilt and patched up with the old decorations, probably during the reigns of William or Anne,* yet still this is the very spot from whence Edward II. dated letters for the arrest of the Knights Templar.

Passing to the back of the house, the view as *home scenery* is all that can be desired. If wings were added to the present house it would form a charming dwelling, for nature has decked the site with exceeding care. The bridge, leading to Byfleet Mill, would delight the 'water-colour men' who like brilliant and broad effects; the Wey in that spot creates little bays, and picturesque 'aites' crowded with charming water-foliage, broad leaves, spiry rushes, and floating islands of forget-me-nots repeating the blue sky of heaven. There is a wild-looking keeper's lodge on an eminence, which we were assured commanded a delicious view, and from which the mill and the mill-house on its flowery island were seen to great advantage, but the autumn sun was going down, and warned us to return. At the back of the dwelling, where the inequalities of the turf seem as if much that was mysterious lay beneath its surface, a subterraneous communication, perhaps with the house, has been discovered; the entrance is arched, and farther on a hole has been dug into it, proving its continuance; it might or might not be worth the trouble of excavation, but it is difficult to resist the desire to

T[illegible]am

* This is very perceptible, both within and without; the traces of modernisation on the *façade* do not conceal the few enrichments of an earlier period, while withinside, there is much carved work, and decorated panelling.

investigate a subterraneous passage of any kind, and the more impracticable it seems the more the desire increases ; we could not learn that any relics of old times have been found there, but when they are found in our neighbourhood they are seldom preserved with care.

We might extend our walks with profit and enjoyment as far 'Windsor Way,' as we have done in the opposite direction. The church at EGHAM (some three miles off or thereabouts) contains several monuments, of which any church might be proud. Among the more remarkable and interesting are two to the Denham family, one representing a body in the act of rising from the grave, the other telling of the Judge Denham who was twice married. The monument is rather remarkable because of the figure of Sir John Denham, the poet of 'Cooper's Hill,' in baby boyhood ; having seen these memorials of the poet's family, it will be pleasant to prolong our walk over the plashy lowlands that lead to the surpassing loveliness of 'Cooper's Hill,' and the heroic field of Runnymead —heroic inasmuch as

'Peace hath her victories as well as war!'

Cooper's Hill still overlooks the glorious river,—Denham's 'theme,' which he longed to make his 'example.'

'Though deep, yet clear ; though gentle, yet not dull ;
Strong without rage ; without o'erflowing, full.'

The hill yet remains, famous for its beauty, as it has ever been :

'his shoulders and his sides
A shady mantle clothes ; his curled brows
Frown on the gentle stream, which calmly flows,
While winds and storms his lofty forehead beat—
The common fate of all that's high and great!'

Its vicinity to Egham, where repose the poet's ancestors, adds interest to the theme of his song.*

* Sir John Denham, the poet of 'Cooper's Hill,' was born in Dublin in 1615—his father being then Chief Baron of the Irish Exchequer. The poet was an uncompromising loyalist, and was actively engaged in the Civil Wars ; and he relates that some lines written by him coming accidentally under the notice of Charles I., the king advised him to 'write no more,' alleging that 'when men are young, and have little else to do, they might vent the over

The Company of Basket-makers (if there be such a company) have claimed a large portion of the field—where the barons, 'clad in complete steel,' assembled to confer with King John upon the great charter of English freedom, by which, Hume truly but coldly says, 'very important liberties and privileges were either granted or secured to every order of men in the kingdom; to the clergy, to the barons, and to the people'—the Basket-makers, we say, have availed themselves of the low land of Runnymead to cultivate osiers; piles and stacks of 'withies' in

Runnymead.

various stages of utility, for several hundred yards shut out the river from the wayfarer, but as he proceeds they disappear, and Cooper's Hill on the left, the rich flat of Runnymead, the Thames, and the groves of Time-honoured Ankerwyke, on its opposite bank, form together a rich and most interesting picture. It is now nearly an hundred years since it was first proposed to erect

flowings of their fancy that way; but when they were thought fit for more serious employments, if they still persisted in that course, it would look as if they minded not the way to any better.' 'Cooper's Hill' obtained a rapid popularity, Dryden described it as 'the exact standard of good writing;' and 'Denham's strength' was lauded by Pope.

a triumphal column upon Runnymead; but we have sometimes a strange antipathy to do what would seem unavoidable; the monument to the memory of Hampden is a sore proof of the niggardliness of liberals to the liberal; but all monuments to such a man or to such a cause must appear poor; the names 'Hampden' and 'Runnymead' suffice; the green and verdant mead, encircled by the coronet of Cooper's Hill, reposing beneath the sun, and shadowed by the passing cloud, is an object of reverence and beauty, immortalised by the glorious liberty which the bold barons of England forced from a spiritless tyrant.

Though Cooper's Hill has no claim to the sublimity of mountain scenery, its peculiar situation commands a broad expanse of country. It rises abruptly from the Runnymead meadows, and extends its long ridge in a north-westerly direction; the summit is approached by a winding road, which from different points of the ascent progressively unfolds a gorgeous number of fertile views, such as no other country in the world can give

> 'Of hills and dales, and woods, and lawns, and spires,
> And glittering towns, and silver streams.'

We have heard that the views from KINGSWOOD Lodge—the dwelling of the hill—are delicious, and that its conservatory contains an exquisite marble statue of 'Hope.' On the west of Cooper's Hill is the interesting estate of ANKERWYKE PURNISH. Anckerwycke has been for a series of years in the possession of the family of Harcourt. There is a 'meet' of the three shires in this vicinity,—Surrey, Buckinghamshire, and Berkshire. The views from the grounds of ANCKERWYCKE, are said to be of exceeding beauty, and the kindness of its master makes eloquent the poor about his domain. All these things, and the sound of the rippling waters of the Thames, and the song of the myriad birds which congregate in its groves, and the legends* sprung of its antiquity, all contribute to the adornment of the gigantic fact that HERE, King John, sorely against his will, signed

* There is much interest attached to a fine old yew tree, beneath whose shadow tradition says Anna Buleyn met Henry VIII. There is a legend, also, that a dove conveyed a bough of that yew tree in its bill to Germany, where a convent was built to protect the relic of Anckerwyicke; but Germany was abandoned after a time for Spain, where the tree now flourishes, it having been transplanted by the monks.

MAGNA CHARTA! How that single fact fills the soul, and nerves the spirit; how proudly the British birthright throbs within our bosoms. We long to lead the new Napoleon, the absolute Nicholas, the frank, hospitable, and brave, but sometimes over-confident American, to this green sward of Runnymead, and tell them that HERE was secured to the Englishman—a LIBERTY *which other nations have never enjoyed!* Here in the thickset beauty of yon little island, was our CHARTER granted. As to how we have kept it, and how enlarged it, 'by God and our country' we may be tried! But surely there is stern truth as well as true poetry in that passage of our Anthem which tells us that

> 'The nations not so blest as thee,
> Must in their turn to tyrants fall,
> Whilst thou shalt flourish great and free,
> The pride and envy of them all!'

There has been much dispute as to whether the Charter was signed upon the Mead or on the Island called '*Magna Charter Island*,' which forms a charming feature in the landscape, and upon which is built a little sort of *altar-house*, so to call it. We leave the settlement of such matters to wiser and more learned heads; but we incline to the idea that John would have felt even the mimic ferry a protection. The island looks even now *exclusive*, and as we were impelled to its shore, we indulged the belief that the charter was really there signed by the king. There was a poetic feeling in whoever planted the bank of 'Forget-me-not' just at the entrance to the low apartment which was fitted up to contain the *charter stone*, by the late Simon Harcourt, Esq., in the year 1835. The inscription on the stone is as follows:—'Be it remembered, that on this island, in June, 1215, JOHN, KING OF ENGLAND, SIGNED THE MAGNA CHARTA, and in the year 1834, this building was erected in commemoration of that great and important event by George Simon Harcourt, Esq., Lord of the Manor and then High Sheriff of the county.' A gentleman rents the island from Mr. Harcourt, and has built there a Gothic cottage in excellent keeping with the place. It adjoins the altar-room, but does not interfere with it, nor with the privilege so graciously bestowed on the public by Mr. Harcourt,—permitting patriots or fishermen to visit the island, and pic-nic in a tent prepared for the purpose, under the shelter of some superb walnut trees.

Though our varied pilgrimage draws to a close, let not our friends imagine there is

'No more to see, no more to tell.'

There is much within a walk of our little pensive town, which we have not recorded, but which we hope we may induce others to record hereafter.

Our Surrey Hills and our Surrey Vales are, in truth, beautiful; but their beauty is enhanced by the many associations of glory that are inseparably and for ever linked with them.

Especially, and above all, be it remembered, that from every ascent to which, in this our Pilgrimage, we have made reference, we obtain a view of Royal WINDSOR, perpetually reminding us, that while, on the one hand, we 'hold fast' the liberties that have been obtained for us by arms or eloquence, on the other we are preserved alike from the evils that Despotism creates, and the perils that arise out of Democracy. And surely, while we raise our hearts to God in thankfulness that the land about us is free as well as fertile, we may waft a blessing towards that regal dwelling, whence, over all the kingdom and its dependencies, a holy and happy influence issues and spreads—teaching goodness by example alike to the high and to the humble, and showing that nowhere, either in palace or in cottage, are the duties of life more wisely or more purely performed than they are in THE ROYAL FAMILY OF ENGLAND.

THE END.

LONDON:
BRADBURY AND EVANS, PRINTERS, WHITEFRIARS.

CPSIA information can be obtained at www.ICGtesting.com
Printed in the USA
BVOW07s1151030614

355265BV00010B/366/P